EVERYDAY
Urbanism

featuring

JOHN CHASE · MARGARET CRAWFORD

WALTER HOOD · MONA HOUGHTON · JOHN KALISKI

DENNIS KEELEY · BARBARA KIRSHENBLATT-GIMBLETT

NORMAN MILLAR · CAMILO JOSE VERGARA · PHOEBE WALL WILSON

EVERYDAY
Urbanism

edited by John Chase, Margaret Crawford, and John Kaliski

THE MONACELLI PRESS

First published in the United States of America in 1999 by

THE MONACELLI PRESS, INC.

10 East 92nd Street, New York, New York 10128

This project was supported by a grant from the
Graham Foundation for Advanced Studies in the Fine Arts
and by the
Los Angeles Forum for Architecture and Urban Design

Library of Congress Cataloging-in-Publication Data
Everyday urbanism : featuring John Chase . . . /
edited by John Chase, Margaret Crawford, and John Kaliski.
p. cm.
Includes bibliographical references.
ISBN 1-885254-81-4
1. Architecture—Human factors—California—Los Angeles.
2. Architecture, Modern—20th century—Social aspects—California—Los Angeles.
3. City planning—United States—History—20th century.
I. Chase, John, date. II. Crawford, Margaret, date. III. Kaliski, John.
NA9053.H76E94   1999
709'.794'94—dc21   99-23898

Printed in Hong Kong

Designed by
Lorraine Wild, Ninotchka Regets, Amanda Washburn, and Snow Kahn

Cover photograph by
Dennis Keeley

Joyfully dedicated to
Francesca Lamei Cenzatti
and
Ana Xiao Fei Wild Kaliski

ACKNOWLEDGMENTS

Many people contributed to this book during its prolonged period of gestation. The original idea of organizing a symposium responding to the Los Angeles Museum of Contemporary Art's exhibition "Urban Revisions: Current Projects for the Public Realm" began with a series of discussions at the Los Angeles Forum for Architecture and Urban Design. These conversations included Julie Silliman, Kris Miller, and Rick Corsini. At MOCA, Elizabeth Smith, the curator of "Urban Revisions," graciously endorsed the idea; the Architecture and Design Council helped fund it; and Caroline Blackburn and Vas Prabhu of the Education Department helped make it a reality. Titled "Above and Below: Urban Design, Urban Theory, and Urban Culture," the symposium was held on May 14, 1994. Kristen Ross, Diana Balmori, Alan Sekula, Ruben Martinez, Mike Davis, Maria Patricia Fernandez-Kelly, Michael Dear, Diane Ghirardo, Paula Sirola, and Michael Sorkin all presented provocative ideas and generated stimulating debate about the current state of urban design. This convinced us that the still-nebulous concept of everyday urbanism addressed crucial gaps in the urban design discourse and should be developed further.

A grant from the Graham Foundation for Advanced Studies in the Fine Arts made the next step, collecting and editing these essays, possible. We are very grateful to the Publications Committee of the Los Angeles Forum (Pat Morton, Chava Danielson, John Dutton, Jonathan Evans, Steven Flusty, Ron Golan, Kris Miller, Deborah Murphy, Kevin V. O'Brian, and Paul Tang) for sponsoring this volume as part of their publications program and particularly to Julie Silliman, who was an invaluable facilitator.

Graphic designer Lorraine Wild joined the project at an early stage and her contribution went far beyond the usual role of the designer. Without her sophisticated understanding of everydayness, her valuable editorial input, and, not least, her incomparable design skills, this book would never have seen the light of day. We can never repay the enormous debt we owe her. Thanks also to her hard-working colleagues at Lorraine Wild Design, Ninotchka Regrets, Amanda Washburn, and Snow Kahn. Dennis Keeley deserves special thanks for generously undertaking a photo essay especially for this book. At The Monacelli Press, we are grateful to Gianfranco Monacelli for immediately understanding the value of the book and to Andrea Monfried for her patient and heroic efforts in finally getting it produced. Particular thanks go to Jen Bilik for her inspired editorial expertise and her belief in clear prose. Finally, we want to thank Michael Rotondi and SCI-Arc for their valuable institutional support. Michael always encouraged our efforts to develop these ideas in seminars and design studios. The SCI-Arc students who took these courses also made significant contributions. Their spirited participation and creative imagination took us a long way in transforming these ideas into reality.

INTRODUCTION

Margaret Crawford

But we are unable to seize the human facts. We fail to see them where
they are, namely in humble, familiar, everyday objects. Our search
for the human takes us too far, too deep. We seek it in the clouds or
in mysteries, whereas it is waiting for us, besieging us on all sides.

—Henri Lefebvre, *The Same and the Other*

What do we mean by everyday urbanism? These two words—one ordinary, the other
obscure—together identify a new position in understanding and approaching the city.
Rather than urban design, urban planning, urban studies, urban theory, or other specialized
terms, urbanism identifies a broad discursive arena that combines all of these disciplines
as well as others into a multidimensional consideration of the city. Cities are inexhaustible
and contain so many overlapping and contradictory meanings—aesthetic, intellectual, physical, social, political, economic, and experiential—that they can never be reconciled into
a single understanding. Urbanism is thus inherently a contested field. The term also carries
with it important echoes of the sociologist Louis Wirth's famous essay title and characterization "Urbanism as a Way of Life."[1] This formulation emphasizes the primacy of human
experience as the fundamental aspect of any definition of urbanism.

"Everyday" speaks to this element of ordinary human experience and itself conveys many
complicated meanings. At a common-sense level, everyday describes the lived experience
shared by urban residents, the banal and ordinary routines we know all too well—commuting,
working, relaxing, moving through city streets and sidewalks, shopping, buying and eating
food, running errands. Even in this descriptive incarnation, the everyday city has rarely
been the focus of attention for architects or urban designers, despite the fact that an
amazing number of social, spatial, and aesthetic meanings can be found in the repeated
activities and conditions that constitute our daily, weekly, and yearly routines. The
utterly ordinary reveals a fabric of space and time defined by a complex realm of social
practices—a conjuncture of accident, desire, and habit.

1
"Urbanism as
a Way of Life,"
first published in
1938, has been
extensively
reprinted. See
Albert J. Reiss,
ed., ON CITIES AND
SOCIAL LIFE (Chicago:
University of
Chicago Press,
1938); and Richard
Sennett, ed.,
CLASSIC ESSAYS ON
THE CULTURE OF
CITIES (Englewood
Cliffs, N.J.: Prentice
Hall, 1969). For a
discussion of other
meanings of
urbanism, see Nan
Ellin, POSTMODERN
URBANISM (New York:
Basil Blackwell,
1996), 225.

The concept of everyday space delineates the physical domain of everyday public activity. Existing in between such defined and physically identifiable realms as the home, the workplace, and the institution, everyday urban space is the connective tissue that binds daily lives together. Everyday space stands in contrast to the carefully planned, officially designated, and often underused spaces of public use that can be found in most American cities. These monumental public spaces only punctuate the larger and more diffuse landscape of everyday life, which tends to be banal and repetitive, everywhere and nowhere, obvious yet invisible. Ambiguous like all in-between spaces, the everyday represents a zone of social transition and possibility with the potential for new social arrangements and forms of imagination.[2]

BETWEEN PHILOSOPHY AND COMMON SENSE

Although the incoherence of everyday space might seem to defeat any conceptual or physical order, the concepts of everyday life as identified by Henri Lefebvre, Guy Debord, and Michel de Certeau serve as an introduction to this rich repository of urban meaning. These three French theorists, all of whom died in the last decade, were, respectively, a Marxist philosopher and sociologist, a filmmaker and would-be revolutionary, and an anthropologist and historian. Pioneers in investigating the completely ignored spheres of daily existence, their work identified the everyday as a crucial arena of modern culture and society. While acknowledging the oppression of daily life, each discovered its potential as a site of creative resistance and liberatory power. In contrast to the French theorists such as Jacques Derrida and Michel Foucault, who dominated academic and architectural discourse over the last two decades, Lefebvre, Debord, and de Certeau insisted on the connection between theory and social practices, between thought and lived experience. Lefebvre pointed out that "when the philosopher turns back towards real life, general concepts which have been worked out by means of a highly specialized activity and abstracted from everyday life are not lost. On the contrary, they take on a new meaning for lived experience."[3] All of the authors included in this book share with these three philosophical predecessors similar assumptions about everyday life.

The belief that everyday life is important governs our work. Lefebvre was the first philosopher to insist that the apparently trivial everyday actually constitutes the basis of all social experience and the true realm of political contestation. Lefebvre described daily life as the "screen on which society projects its light and its shadow, its hollows and its planes, its power and its weakness."[4] In spite of this significance, Lefebvre warns, the everyday is

2
For Victor Turner's concept of liminality, "betwixt and between," see THE FOREST OF SYMBOLS (Ithaca, N.Y.: Cornell University Press, 1967), 93–110. Also see Donald Weber on the related concept of "border," in "From Limen to Border: A Meditation on the Legacy of Victor Turner for American Cultural Studies," AMERICAN QUARTERLY 47 (September 1995): 525–37.

3
Henri Lefebvre, CRITIQUE OF EVERYDAY LIFE (London: Verso, 1991), 95.

4
Lefebvre, CRITIQUE OF EVERYDAY LIFE, 18.

difficult to decode due to its fundamental ambiguity. As the first step in analyzing this slippery concept, Lefebvre distinguished between two simultaneous realities that exist within everyday life: the *quotidian*, the timeless, humble, repetitive natural rhythms of life; and the *modern*, the always new and constantly changing habits that are shaped by technology and worldliness.[5] Lefebvre structured his analysis of everyday life around this duality, looking past potentially alienating aspects in an effort to unearth the deeply human elements that still exist within the everyday. While most urbanists influenced by Lefebvre have critiqued modernity's negative effects on the city,[6] we have tried optimistically to focus on the other side of the equation—the possibility of reclaiming elements of the quotidian that have been hidden in the nooks and crannies of the urban environment. We have discovered these qualities in overlooked, marginal places, from streets and sidewalks to vacant lots and parks, from suburbia to the inner city.

We believe that lived experience should be more important than physical form in defining the city. This perspective distinguishes us from many designers and critics who point to the visual incoherence of everyday space as exemplifying everything that is wrong with American cities. Like Lefebvre, Debord, and de Certeau, we understand urbanism to be a human and social discourse. The city is, above all, a social product, created out of the demands of everyday use and the social struggles of urban inhabitants. Design within everyday space must start with an understanding and acceptance of the life that takes place there. This goes against the grain of professional design discourse, which is based on abstract principles, whether quantitative, formal, spatial, or perceptual. Whatever the intention, professional abstractions inevitably produce spaces that have little to do with real human impulses. We agree with Raymond Ledrut's conclusion "The problem today—which has nothing 'philosophical' about it—is that of the real life 'of' the city and 'in' the city. The true issue is not to make beautiful cities or well-managed cities, it is to make a work of life. The rest is a by-product."[7]

For us, the play of difference is the primary element in the "real life" of the city. Lefebvre observed that abstract urban spaces, primarily designed to be reproduced, "negated all differences, those that come from nature and history as well as those that come from the body, ages, sexes, and ethnicities."[8] This is visible everywhere in increasingly generic yet specialized spaces that parcel daily experience into separate domains. Though difference is progressively negated in urban space, however, it nonetheless remains the most salient fact of everyday life. Its burdens and pleasures are distributed unevenly, according to class, age, race, and gender. Lefebvre focused particular attention on the victims of everyday life,

5
Henri Lefebvre, EVERYDAY LIFE IN THE MODERN WORLD (New York: Harper, 1971), 25.

6
See, for example, Kristen Ross, FAST CARS AND CLEAN BODIES (Cambridge, Mass.: MIT Press, 1995); Edward Soja, POSTMODERN GEOGRAPHIES (London: Verso, 1989), and THIRDSPACE: JOURNEYS TO LOS ANGELES AND OTHER REAL AND IMAGINED PLACES (New York: Blackwell, 1996); and Mark Gottdeiner, THE SOCIAL PRODUCTION OF URBAN SPACE (Austin: University of Texas Press, 1985).

7
Raymond Ledrut, "Speech and the Silence of the City," in THE CITY AND THE SIGN: AN INTRODUCTION TO URBAN SEMIOTICS, ed. Mark Gottdeiner and Alexandros Langopoulos (New York: Columbia University Press, 1986), 133.

8
Henri Lefebvre, "Space: Social Product and Use Value," in CRITICAL SOCIOLOGY: EUROPEAN PERSPECTIVES, ed. J. W. Freiberg (New York: Irvington, 1979), 289.

especially women sentenced to endless routines of housework and shopping. Lefebvre also identified immigrants, low-level employees, and teenagers as victims of everyday life, although "never in the same way, never at the same time, never all at once."[9]

9
Lefebvre, CRITIQUE OF EVERYDAY LIFE, 127.

To locate these differences physically in everyday lives is to map the social geography of the city. The city of the bus rider or pedestrian does not resemble that of the automobile owner. A shopping cart means very different things to a busy mother in a supermarket and a homeless person on the sidewalk. These differences separate the lives of urban inhabitants from one another, while their overlap constitutes the primary form of social exchange in the city. The intersections between an individual or defined group and the rest of the city are everyday space—the site of multiple social and economic transactions, where multiple experiences accumulate in a single location. These places where differences collide or interact are the most potent sites for everyday urbanism.

The goal of everyday urbanism is to orchestrate what the literary theorist Mikhail Bakhtin called "dialogism." A mode of textual analysis, dialogism can easily be applied to design practices. Bakhtin defined dialogism as the characteristic epistemological mode of a world dominated by "heteroglossia"—the constant interaction between meanings, all of which can potentially influence the others. "Dialogization" occurs when a word, discourse, language, or culture becomes relativized, deprivileged, and aware of competing definitions for the same things. Undialogized language remains authoritarian or absolute.[10] To dialogize design in the city challenges the conceptual hierarchy under which most design professionals operate. Everyday life provides a good starting point for this shift because it is grounded in the commonplace rather than the canonical, the many rather than the few, and the repeated rather than the unique; and it is uniquely comprehensible to ordinary people.

10
Mikhail Bakhtin, THE DIALOGIC IMAGINATION: FOUR ESSAYS, ed. Michael Holmquist (Austin: University of Texas Press, 1981), 426–27.

Not surprisingly, since everyone is potentially an expert on everyday life, everyday life has never been of much interest to experts. Lefebvre pointed out that although experts and intellectuals are embedded in everyday life, they prefer to think of themselves as outside and elsewhere. Convinced that everyday life is trivial, they attempt to evade it. They use rhetoric and metalanguage as "permanent substitutes for experience, allowing them to ignore the mediocrity of their own condition."[11] Lefebvre also described the purpose of such distancing techniques: "Abstract culture places an almost opaque screen (if it were completely opaque the situation would be simpler) between cultivated [people] and everyday life. Abstract culture not only supplies them with words and ideas but also with an attitude which forces them to seek the 'meaning' of their lives and consciousness outside of themselves and their real relations with the world."[12]

11
Lefebvre, EVERYDAY LIFE IN THE MODERN WORLD, 92.

12
Lefebvre, CRITIQUE OF EVERYDAY LIFE, 238.

To avoid this breach with reality, everyday urbanism demands a radical repositioning of the designer, a shifting of power from the professional expert to the ordinary person. Widespread expertise in everyday life acts as a leveling agent, eliminating the distance between professionals and users, between specialized knowledge and daily experience. The designer is immersed within contemporary society rather than superior to and outside it, and is thus forced to address the contradictions of social life from close up.

TIME AND SPACE

Both Michel de Certeau and Henri Lefebvre argued that the temporal is as significant as the spatial in everyday life. De Certeau drew a distinction between two modes of operation: strategies, based on place, and tactics, based on time. Strategies represent the practices of those in power, postulating "a place that can be delimited as its own and serve as the base from which relations with an exteriority composed of targets or threats can be managed." Strategies establish a "proper" place, either spatial or institutional, such that place triumphs over time. Political, economic, and scientific rationalities are constructed on the strategic model. In contrast, a tactic is a way of operating without a proper place, and so depends on time. As a result, tactics lack the borders necessary for designation as visible totalities: "The place of a tactic belongs to the other." Tactics are the "art of the weak," incursions into the field of the powerful. Without a proper place, tactics rely on seized opportunities, on cleverly chosen moments, and on the rapidity of movements that can change the organization of a space. Tactics are a form of everyday creativity. Many of the urban activities we describe are tactical. By challenging the "proper" places of the city, this range of transitory, temporary, and ephemeral urban activities constitutes counterpractices to officially sanctioned urbanisms.

Lefebvre also identified another set of multiple temporalities composing urban life. Everyday time is located at the intersection of two contrasting but coexisting modes of repetition, the cyclical and the linear. The cyclical consists of the rhythms of nature: night and day, changing seasons, birth and death. Rational processes define linear patterns, time measured into quantifiable schedules of work and leisure with such units as timetables, fast food, coffee breaks, and prime time. Repeated across days, weeks, months, years, and life-times, these competing rhythms shape our lived experience. More important to Lefebvre than these predictable oscillations, however, is a third category of time, the discontinuous and spontaneous moments that punctuate daily experience—fleeting sensations of love, play, rest, knowledge. These instants of rupture and illumination, arising from everyone's daily existence, reveal the possibilities and limitations of life.[13] They highlight the distance

13
Henri Lefebvre,
LA SOMME ET LE
RESTE, VOL. 2 (Paris:
La Nef de Paris,
1959), discussed
in David Harvey,
"Afterword" in
Henri Lefebvre,
THE PRODUCTION OF
SPACE (New York:
Blackwell, 1991),
429.

between what life is and what it might be. Although these moments quickly pass into oblivion, they provide the key to the powers contained in the everyday and function as starting points for social change. Guy Debord saw them as potential revolutions in individual everyday life, springboards for the realization of the possible.[14] By recognizing and building on these understandings of time, we can explore new and barely acknowledged realms of urban experience.

THE POLITICS OF EVERYDAY LIFE

Like these writers, we want to draw attention to the transformational possibilities of the everyday. Alice Kaplan and Kristen Ross have pointed out that the political is hidden within the contradictions and possibilities of lived experience.[15] The most banal and repetitive gestures of everyday life give rise to desires that cannot be satisfied there. If these desires could acquire a political language, they would make a new set of personal and collective demands on the social order. Therefore the practices of everyday urbanism should inevitably lead to social change, not via abstract political ideologies imposed from outside, but instead through specific concerns that arise from the lived experience of different individuals and groups in the city.

While acknowledging our debts to Lefebvre and Debord, the general position of writers included in this book is not identical to theirs. Both Lefebvre and Debord identified the urban environment as a unique site for contesting the alienation of modern capitalist society and believed that this alienation could be overcome, thus rendering individuals whole once again. They saw both the society they attacked and the future society they desired as totalities.[16] We instead acknowledge fragmentation and incompleteness as inevitable conditions of postmodern life. We do not seek overarching solutions. There is no universal everyday urbanism, only a multiplicity of responses to specific times and places. Our solutions are modest and small in scale—micro-utopias, perhaps, contained in a sidewalk, a bus bench, or a minipark. In a rare nontotalizing moment, Debord declared that "One day, we will construct cities for drifting . . . but, with light retouching, one can utilize certain zones which already exist. One can utilize certain persons who already exist."[17] One purpose of this book is to identify a few of those zones and a few of those persons.

TOWARD EVERYDAY URBANISM

The possibility that the concept of everyday urbanism might interest a broader audience first became apparent to the editors in 1994, when we organized a symposium as part of

14
Guy Debord, "Preliminary Problems in Constructing a Situation," in Ken Knabb, SITUATIONIST INTERNATIONAL ANTHOLOGY (Berkeley: Bureau of Public Secrets, 1981), 43–45.

15
Alice Kaplan and Kristen Ross, introduction to Everyday Life issue of YALE FRENCH STUDIES 73 (fall 1987): 4.

16
For further discussions of the concept of totality see Martin Jay, MARXISM AND TOTALITY: THE ADVENTURES OF A CONCEPT FROM LUKAS TO HABERMAS (Berkeley: University of California Press, 1984), 276–99; and Peter Wollen, "Bitter Victory: The Art and Politics of the Situationist International," in ON THE PASSAGE OF A FEW PEOPLE THROUGH A BRIEF MOMENT IN TIME, ed. Elizabeth Sussman (Cambridge, Mass.: MIT Press, 1989).

17
Guy Debord, "La Théorie de la dérive," in LES LEVRES NUES 9 (November 1956): 10.

the Los Angeles Museum of Contemporary Art's "Urban Revisions" exhibition. From this symposium we began to assemble the book, which took shape slowly through heated but always stimulating discussions, our attempts to delineate the amorphous contours of everyday life. This project is the product of our friendship; each of us brought different interests, perspectives, and knowledge to this collaborative endeavor. We discovered around us other writers, photographers, and architects working with similar ideas. Though much of the work described here takes place in Los Angeles, we hope that the relevance of these ideas and activities extends into the general realm of the urban. We suspect that this book represents only a small glimpse at everyday urbanism, and that multiple versions already exist across the country, ripe for further examination.[18]

18
See, for example, Deborah Berke and Steven Harris, eds., ARCHITECTURE OF THE EVERYDAY (New York: Princeton Architectural Press, 1997).

The book divides into two sections, "Looking at the City" and "Making the City." The first group of essays examines a range of existing activities and places around Los Angeles and New York. Sanctioned yet unofficial, highly visible but hidden, these underexplored places have important things to say. Barbara Kirshenblatt-Gimblett observes street activities in New York City, from parades to children at play, and argues that such vernacular performances constitute a type of architecture because they give form to urban space. In new kinds of public spaces that are produced by such everyday activities as garage sales and street vending in Los Angeles, I see multiple publics asserting their identities and delineating new urban arenas for political action. Mona Houghton describes a very different social context in Los Angeles, the bohemian enclave of Laurel Canyon, where Ernest Rosenthal, scavenger and recycler, tends his continuously evolving garden. Too sophisticated to be an outsider but more obsessed than the typical home gardener, Rosenthal challenges distinctions between high and low. Dennis Keeley's photo essay reveals the beauty and humor of Rosenthal's garden. John Chase focuses on his own Southern California neighborhood, Venice, to analyze trash as a mode of urban information and communication, a medium through which urban residents understand and attempt to control their environment. Finally, Camilo José Vergara's portfolio of photographs surveys economic activities in South Central Los Angeles, documenting the ways in which Hispanic immigrants transform their public environment, visible on streets and fences as well as in garages and yards.

The second half of the book looks at design activities, professionals collaborating in building the everyday city. John Kaliski provides theoretical context by tracing the history of everyday urbanism within the postmodern discourse of urban design. Urban designers, argues Kaliski, have consistently evaded the realities of existing urban life, by attempting either to recover the past or to control the future. He proposes everyday urbanism as an alternative to the failure of the abstract modernist city. In the next two essays, John Chase and Phoebe Wall Wilson present small-scale projects that respond practically to daily life in two very different Los Angeles municipalities, West Hollywood and Pasadena. Both projects retrofit single-use environments with multiple functions and amenities to encourage spontaneous social interaction. Both projects, conceived within existing planning and regulatory frameworks, are very likely to be implemented. Norman Millar describes the satisfactions and frustrations of his ongoing work with Central American street vendors in MacArthur Park. The relationship between the professional designers, the vendors, and the city is intermittent and rarely conclusive, challenging existing modes of architectural practice. Walter Hood uses an improvisatory method to re-create conceptually a minipark and its surrounding streets in West Oakland. Hood imagines responses to the multiple needs of the entire neighborhood, redesigning the park to accommodate beer drinkers, recyclers, and prostitutes as well as gardeners and children. Finally, "Quotidian Bricolage" is a collection of student design projects based on everyday life in ordinary places. The imaginative transformations of unpromising sites, ranging from the concrete banks of the Los Angeles River to the generic strip mall to the Culver City bus system, demonstrate the potential of everyday urbanism as an alternative design-studio pedagogy.

In spite of its detailed discussion of theoretical influences, this book was written not as a scholarly or critical work but primarily as a call to action. Unifying the ideas and practices of everyday urbanism presented here is the hope that all might serve as entry points for an understanding of everyday space and as incentives for rethinking the ways in which designers can operate there. Proposing alternatives to the limited scope and methods of contemporary urban design, these essays attempt to reconnect design to human, social, and political concerns without repeating the narrow, deterministic approaches of the social and advocacy architecture movements of the 1960s. Instead, everyday urbanism seeks to release the powers of creativity and imagination already present within daily life as the means of transforming urban experience and the city.

Part 1

LOOKING
at the City

PERFORMING THE CITY: REFLECTIONS ON THE URBAN VERNACULAR

Barbara Kirshenblatt-Gimblett

The limits of planning and design can be learned from the vernacular. Community participation in a planning process is not enough. The place of the urban vernacular—of architecture without architects and urban space without planning—is the urban revision on exhibition.

The vernacular is what ordinary people do in their everyday lives. It consists of local practices that take shape outside planning, design, zoning, regulation, and covenants, if not in spite of them. The relationship between the built environment and the social practices that occur within it reveal both intentional and unintentional effects of great importance. The vernacular can help us discover what cannot—indeed, what should not—be planned. It can suggest what should be protected from design and should be left to its own devices, free to find its own spatial form.

Michel de Certeau's distinction between the strategic and the tactical defines the difference between urban planning and the urban vernacular.[1] It is not by accident that design projects designate themselves "master" plan or "strategic" plan. Think of the vernacular as the opposite: not a master plan, but a local improvisation; not a strategic plan, but a tactical strike.

Performance is also central to the production of the urban vernacular, for performance produces spatial form. By performance I mean everything from hanging the laundry out to dry to hopscotch or lion dancing during the Chinese New Year holiday. Activities produce distinctive spatial forms, some of which acquire independent architectural manifestations. The New York Stock Exchange is one such example. Bidders used to transact their deals in

1
Michel de Certeau,
THE PRACTICE
OF EVERYDAY LIFE
(Berkeley and
Los Angeles:
University of
California
Press, 1988).

small circles on the docks and streets of lower Manhattan. Older spatial practices came indoors, and even in this age of information technology traders stand around pits in the exchange and continue live bidding, much as they once did outside.

Design operates from the premise of a designated and secure space. Because the urban vernacular is instead by its very nature tactical, the spatial practices of the lived city have a very temporal character. Street performers and vendors or children at play occupy space precariously. They must be ready to move at a moment's notice. The tactical is an improvisational art, which is why attempts to plan, regulate, or zone such activities are questionable. The history of the playground, a space designed to relocate children from the street to an area that adults can supervise, might be seen as part of the larger history of organized play. No space designed for play is as interesting as the life-world.

Nor can such control—auditioning street musicians and designating places and times for them to perform, or moving vendors away from heavily trafficked areas—produce vibrant public spaces. Washington Square Park in Manhattan is one such place, never designed for the many activities that take place there. On a weekend with nice weather, thousands of strangers gather at the park and produce a complex ensemble performance without plans, sponsoring organizations, funding, publicity, or announced schedules.

Tacit understanding is what governs this multiform space, as it does New York City's Easter Parade, which is not a parade but a fashion promenade. For more than a century, this event has occurred without fail every Easter Sunday between noon and two o'clock on Fifth Avenue in the vicinity of St. Patrick's Cathedral. There are no announcements, no planning or preparation. Tens of thousands of people just show up. The police know to erect traffic barricades. And for about two hours, the enormous crowd mills about, seeing and being seen in their Easter finery.

This kind of event represents the epitome of one form of the urban vernacular—namely, the success of enormous numbers of strangers in producing an improvised ensemble performance on the basis of tacit understanding in a space not designated for the purpose. Ephemeral as they may seem, events like the Easter Parade or the St. Patrick's Day Parade, which dates to the mid–eighteenth century, have outlasted many buildings in the city. These events indicate the effectiveness with which people, even complete strangers, can act in concert, a cohesiveness that cannot be legislated or designed, though certainly some designs are inimical to such activity while others are conducive to it.

These activities are themselves architectural in the sense that performance (broadly conceived) gives form to space. This is space constituted in performance. Space thus adapted is different from staging the city as theater, treating an urban setting as a stage set (for example, lighting it theatrically). The performance itself is architectural. It depends more on repetition, reenactment, and renewal than on permanent materialization. Perhaps this is why vernacular performances so often take place in the life-world rather than in designated spaces such as theaters, bandshells, or playgrounds.

Created from sound, smoke, and bodies, the lion-dance processions in the streets of Manhattan's Chinatown offer a brilliant example of performance architecture. On the Chinese New Year, as many as twelve martial clubs at a time map out their own routes through what has become the ceremonial center of the Chinese community in the metropolitan area. Led by supporters carrying the club banner, dancers wearing full-body lion masks perform at store entrances to usher in a good year. Shopkeepers set out food for the lions in advance and reward the performers with little red envelopes of money for their cleverness in retrieving the symbolic sustenance. For a few minutes or for almost an hour, depending on how much they will be paid, the performers carve out a space in the life-world even as business and traffic proceed as usual. Sound defines the outer limits of the performance space, the area within earshot as delineated by the continuous percussion of drums and brass gongs and punctuated by deafening explosions of firecrackers that mark the end of a performance.

The smoke of the firecrackers is ambient architecture, a wall of opaque witness that extends as far as the eye can see and the nose can smell. As the smoke slowly dissipates, sunlight filters through the haze, illuminating the space of the street in a distinctive way. By the end of the day, smoke still lingers in the air. Sidewalks and roads are lined with the firecrackers' shredded red paper. While the clubs now seek permits for their processions and some streets are closed to traffic, the rules are relaxed, and laws are selectively enforced. Firecrackers are illegal in New York City, but are everywhere during the celebrations.

Performance is also an instrument of urban memory, the body its archive. Landmarking and historic preservation materialize memory on a site, whether by conserving, restoring, or re-creating a building, or by installing a plaque to mark its absence. Vernacular memory works in other ways—in shrines, sidewalk altars, memorial walls, and gardens, and in performances that represent an architecture created from the archive of the body. These are the "lieux des mémoires" that Pierre Nora writes about.[2] Their very proliferation is a symptom of the fear of forgetting, a delegation of memory responsibilities to museums, libraries, memorials, and historic districts.

2
Pierre Nora,
"Between Memory
and History:
Les Lieux des
Mémoires,"
REPRESENTATIONS 26
(spring 1989): 7.

BLURRING THE BOUNDARIES:
PUBLIC SPACE
AND PRIVATE LIFE

Margaret Crawford

This investigation originated in my dissatisfaction with a critical position that emerged in architectural discourse a few years ago. Critics and historians began to see multiple versions of the theme park in the increasingly spectacular and centralized zones of leisure and consumption—gentrified shopping streets, massive shopping malls, festival marketplaces. According to Michael Sorkin, one of the primary theorists in this arena, these ersatz and privatized pieces of the city—pseudopublic places—were distinguished by consumption, surveillance, control, and endless simulation. I include my own work among this body of criticism; I contributed a chapter concluding that the entire world had become a gigantic shopping mall to Sorkin's book *Variations on a Theme Park: The New American City and the End of Public Space*.[1]

What concerned me more than the emerging theme-park sensibility as depicted in these studies was part of the book's subtitle, "The End of Public Space." This summarizes a fear repeated by many other critics, urbanists, and architects; in his essay in Sorkin's book, Mike Davis expresses alarm at the "destruction of any truly democratic urban spaces."[2] It is easy to find evidence to support this argument. Los Angeles, for example, is often cited as an extreme demonstration of the decline of public space. The few remaining slices of traditional public space (for example, Pershing Square, historically the focus of the downtown business district, which was recently redesigned by Ricardo Legorreta) are usually deserted, while Citywalk, the simulated cityscape, shopping, and entertainment center collaged from different urban elements by MCA and Universal Studio, is always jammed with people.

1
Michael Sorkin, ed., VARIATIONS ON A THEME PARK: THE NEW AMERICAN CITY AND THE END OF PUBLIC SPACE (New York: Hill and Wang, 1990)

2
Mike Davis, "Fortress Los Angeles: The Militarization of Urban Space," in Sorkin, VARIATIONS ON A THEME PARK, 155.

The existence and popularity of these commercial public places is used to frame a pervasive narrative of loss that contrasts the current debasement of public space with golden ages and golden sites—the Greek agora, the coffeehouses of early modern Paris and London, the Italian piazza, the town square. The narrative nostalgically posits these as once vital sites of democracy where, allegedly, cohesive public discourse thrived, and inevitably culminates in the contemporary crisis of public life and public space, a crisis that puts at risk the very ideas and institutions of democracy itself.

It is hard to argue with the symptoms these writers describe, but I disagree with the conclusions they draw. This perception of loss originates in extremely narrow and normative definitions of both "public" and "space" that derive from insistence on unity, desire for fixed categories of time and space, and rigidly conceived notions of private and public. Seeking a single, all-inclusive public space, these critics mistake monumental public spaces for the totality of public space. In this respect, critics of public space closely echo the conclusions of social theorists such as Jürgen Habermas and Richard Sennett, whose descriptions of the public sphere share many of the same assumptions.[3] Habermas describes the public sphere as overwhelmed by consumerism, the media, and the state, while Sennett laments in his book's very title "the fall of public man." The word "man" highlights another key assumption of this position: an inability to conceive of identity in any but universalizing terms. Whether as universal man, citizen, consumer, or tourist, the identified subjects posit a normative condition of experience.

Not surprisingly, the political implications that follow from the overwhelmingly negative assessments of the narrative of loss are equally negative. Implicit is a form of historical determinism that suggests the impossibility of political struggle against what Mike Davis calls "inexorable forces."[4] The universal consumer becomes the universal victim, helpless and passive against the forces of capitalism, consumerism, and simulation. This tyranny is compounded by the lack of a clear link between public space and democracy. The two are assumed to be closely connected, but exact affinities are never specified, which makes it even more difficult to imagine political opposition to the mall or theme park.

This universalization, pessimism, and ambiguity led me to seek an alternative frame-work—a new way of conceptualizing public space and a new way of reading Los Angeles. This essay represents an account of my attempts to rethink our conceptions of "public," "space," and "identity." The investigation revealed to me a multiplicity of simultaneous public activities in Los Angeles that are continually redefining both "public" and "space" through lived experience. In vacant lots, sidewalks, parks, and parking lots, these activities are

3
See Jürgen Habermas, THE STRUCTURAL TRANSFORMATION OF THE PUBLIC SPHERE: AN INQUIRY INTO A CATEGORY OF BOURGEOIS SOCIETY (Cambridge, Mass.: MIT Press, 1989); and Richard Sennett, THE FALL OF PUBLIC MAN (New York: Vintage Books, 1974).

4
Davis, "Fortress Los Angeles," 154-80.

restructuring urban space, opening new political arenas, and producing new forms of insurgent citizenship.

RETHINKING "PUBLIC"

Nancy Fraser's article "Rethinking the Public Sphere" provided an important starting point for my quest.[5] Her central arguments clarify the significant theoretical and political limitations of prevailing formulations of "public." Fraser acknowledges the importance of Jürgen Habermas's characterization of the public sphere as an arena of discursive relations conceptually independent of both the state and the economy, but she questions many of his assumptions about the universal, rational, and noncontentious public arena.

Habermas links the emergence of the "liberal model of the bourgeois public sphere" in early modern Europe with the development of nation-states in which democracy was represented by collectively accepted universal rights and achieved via electoral politics. This version of the public sphere emphasizes unity and equality as ideal conditions. The public sphere is depicted as a "space of democracy" that all citizens have the right to inhabit. In this arena, social and economic inequalities are temporarily put aside in the interest of determining a common good. Matters of common interest are discussed through rational, disinterested, and virtuous public debate. Like the frequently cited ideal of Athenian democracy, however, this model is structured around significant exclusions. In Athens, participation was theoretically open to all citizens, but in practice the majority of the population—women and slaves—were excluded; they were not "citizens." The modern bourgeois public sphere also began by excluding women and workers: women's interests were presumed to be private and therefore part of the domestic sphere, while workers' concerns were presumed to be merely economic and therefore self-interested. Middle-class and masculine modes of public speech and behavior, through the required rational deliberation and rhetoric of disinterest, were privileged and defined as universal.

Recent revisionist histories, notes Fraser, contradict this idealized account, demonstrating that nonliberal, nonbourgeois public spheres also existed, producing their own definitions and public activities in a multiplicity of arenas.[6] For example, in nineteenth- and twentieth-century America, middle-class women organized themselves into a variety of exclusively female volunteer groups for the purposes of philanthropy and reform based on private ideals of domesticity and motherhood. Less affluent women found access to public life through the workplace and through associations including unions, lodges, and political organizations such as Tammany Hall. Broadening the definition of public to encompass

5
Nancy Fraser, "Rethinking the Public Sphere: A Contribution to the Critique of Actually Existing Democracy," in THE PHANTOM PUBLIC SPHERE, ed. Bruce Robbins (Minneapolis: University of Minnesota Press, 1993).

6
Joan Landes, WOMEN AND THE PUBLIC SPHERE IN THE AGE OF THE FRENCH REVOLUTION (Ithaca, N.Y.: Cornell University Press, 1988); Mary P. Ryan, WOMEN IN PUBLIC: BETWEEN BANNERS AND BALLOTS, 1825–1880 (Baltimore: Johns Hopkins University Press, 1990).

these "counterpublics" produces a very different picture of the public sphere, one founded on contestation rather than unity and created through competing interests and violent demands as much as reasoned debate. Demonstrations, strikes, riots, and struggles over such issues as temperance and suffrage reveal a range of discursive sites characterized by multiple publics and varied struggles between contentious concerns.

In the bourgeois public sphere, citizenship is primarily defined in relation to the state, framed within clear categories of discourse, and addressed through political debate and electoral politics. This liberal notion of citizenship is based on abstract universal liberties, with democracy guaranteed by the state's electoral and juridical institutions. Fraser argues instead that democracy is a complex and contested concept that can assume a multiplicity of meanings and forms that often violate the strict lines between private and public on which the liberal bourgeois public sphere depends. In the United States, counterpublics of women, workers, and immigrants have historically defended established civil rights but also demanded new rights based on their specific roles in the domestic or economic spheres. Always changing, these demands continually redefine democracy and redraw boundaries between private and public.

Fraser's description of multiple publics, contestation, and the redefinition of public and private can be extended to the physical realm of public space. First, these ideas suggest that no single physical environment can represent a completely inclusive space of democracy. Like Habermas's idealized bourgeois public sphere, the physical spaces often idealized by architects—the agora, the forum, the piazza—were constituted by exclusion. Where these single publics are construed as occupying an exemplary public space, the multiple counterpublics that Fraser identifies necessarily require and produce multiple sites of public expression. These spaces are partial and selective in response to the limited segments of the population they serve from among the many public roles that individuals play in urban society.

REDEFINING "SPACE"

In order to locate these multiple sites of public expression, we need to redefine our understanding of "space." Just as Nancy Fraser looked beyond the officially designated public to discover the previously hidden counterpublics of women and workers, we can identify another type of space by looking beyond the culturally defined physical realms of home, workplace, and institution. I call this new construction "everyday space." Everyday space is the connective tissue that binds daily lives together, amorphous and so persuasive that it is difficult even to perceive. In spite of its ubiquity, everyday space is nearly invisible in the professional discourses of the city. Everyday space is like everyday life, the "screen on which society projects its light and its shadow, its hollows and its planes, its power and its weakness."[7]

In the vast expanses of Los Angeles, monumental, highly ordered, and carefully designed public spaces like Pershing Square or Citywalk punctuate the larger and more diffuse space of everyday life. Southern California's banal, incoherent, and repetitive landscape of roads is lined with endless strip malls, supermarkets, auto-repair facilities, fast-food outlets, and vacant lots that defeat any conceptual or physical order. According to Lefebvre, these spaces are like everyday life: "trivial, obvious but invisible, everywhere and nowhere." For most Angelenos, such spaces constitute an everyday reality of infinitely recurring commuting routes and trips to the supermarket, dry cleaner, or video store. The sites for multiple social and economic transactions, these mundane places serve as primary intersections between the individual and the city.

Created to be seen and approached from moving vehicles, this generic landscape exists to accommodate the automobile, which has produced the city's sprawling form. Connected by an expansive network of streets and freeways, Los Angeles spreads out in all directions with few differences of density or form. Experienced through the automobile, the bus, or even the shopping cart, this environment takes mobility as its defining element. Everyday life is organized by time as much as by space, structured around daily itineraries, with rhythms imposed by patterns of work and leisure, week and weekend, and the repetitious gestures of commuting and consumption.

In contrast to the fluidity of its urban fabric, the social fabric of Los Angeles is fragmented; it is not a single city but a collection of microcities defined by visible and invisible boundaries of class, race, ethnicity, and religion. This multiplicity of identities produces an

7
Henri Lefebvre,
CRITIQUE OF
EVERYDAY LIFE
(London: Verso,
1991).

Above: Pershing Square at noon on a weekday
Left: Everyday space in Los Angeles, through the windshield

intricate social landscape in which cultures consolidate and separate, reacting and interacting in complex and unpredictable ways. Spatial and cultural differences exist even within these groups. "Latino," for example, describes the now dominant ethnic group but hides the significant differences between Mexicans and Cubans, for example, or even between recent immigrants and second- or third-generation Chicanos. Mobility prevails here too. When new immigrants arrive from Central America, they tend to move into African American neighborhoods. Both African Americans and Latinos shop in Korean and Vietnamese shops. Other areas of the city, once completely white, then primarily Latino, are now mostly Asian.

These generally distinct groups came together—intensified and politicized—in the urban disturbances of 1992. According to Nancy Fraser's redefinition of the public sphere, these events can be seen as a form of public expression that produces an alternative discourse of "public" and "space." Both the direct causes of the riots and their expression of the riots were embedded in everyday life. For Rodney King, a drive on the freeway ended in a savage beating that shocked the world. The ordinary act of purchasing a bottle of juice in a convenience market after school resulted in Latasha Harlin's death. The verdicts in the Harlin and King trials unleashed a complex outpouring of public concern. Multiple and competing demands (some highly specific, others barely articulated), a spontaneous and undefined moment of public expression, exploded on the streets and sidewalks of Los Angeles. African Americans, many of whom called the uprising the "justice riots," attacked the criminal-justice system. Concepts of universally defined civil rights failed to ameliorate or condemn the visible racism of the Los Angeles Police Department and the court system, which to many constituted a denial of the fundamental rights of citizenship.

The riots dramatized economic issues: poverty, unemployment, and the difficulty of financial self-determination, all exacerbated by recession and long-term effects of deindustrialization. The disturbances also revealed the city's tangled racial dynamics: 51 percent of those arrested were Hispanic (and of that group, most were recent immigrants) while only 34 percent were African American. Immigrants were pitted against one another, and stores owned by Koreans were the focus of much of the burning and looting.

The automobile played a prominent role in the rioting, from the initial act of pulling Reginald Denny from his truck to the rapid expansion of looters who moved across the city by car. Spaces formerly devoted to the automobile—streets, parking lots, swap meets, and strip malls—were temporarily transformed into sites of protest and rage, into new zones of public expression.

EVERYDAY PUBLIC SPACES

The riots underlined the potent ability of everyday spaces to become, however briefly, places where lived experience and political expression come together. This realm of public life lies outside the domain of electoral politics or professional design, representing a bottom-up rather than top-down restructuring of urban space. Unlike normative public spaces, which produce the existing ideology, these spaces help to overturn the status quo. In different areas of the city, generic spaces become specific and serve as public arenas where debates and struggles over economic participation, democracy, and the public assertion of identity take place. Without claiming to represent the totality of public space, these multiple and simultaneous activities construct and reveal an alternative logic of public space.

Woven into the patterns of everyday life, it is difficult even to discern these places as public space. Trivial and commonplace, vacant lots, sidewalks, front yards, parks, and parking lots are being claimed for new uses and meanings by the poor, the recently immigrated, the homeless, and even the middle class. These spaces exist physically somewhere in the junctures between private, commercial, and domestic. Ambiguous and unstable, they blur our established understandings of these categories in often paradoxical ways. They contain multiple and constantly shifting meanings rather than clarity of function. In the absence of a distinct identity of their own, these spaces can be shaped and redefined by the transitory activities they accommodate. Unrestricted by the dictates of built form, they become venues for the expression of new meanings through the individuals and groups who appropriate

The 1992 urban unrest as reported in the
LOS ANGELES TIMES

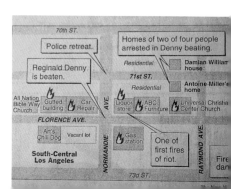

the spaces for their own purposes. Apparently empty of meaning, they acquire constantly changing meanings—social, aesthetic, political, economic—as users reorganize and reinterpret them.

Temporally, everyday spaces exist in between past and future uses, often with a no-longer-but-not-yet-their-own status, in a holding pattern of real-estate values that might one day rise. The temporary activities that take place there also follow distinct temporal patterns. Without fixed schedules, they produce their own cycles, appearing, reappearing, or disappearing within the rhythms of everyday life. Use and activity vary according to the seasons, vanishing in winter, born again in spring. They are subject to changes in the weather, days of the week, and even time of day. Since they are usually perceived in states of distraction, their meanings are not immediately evident but unfold through the repetitious acts of everyday life.

Conceptually, these spaces can be identified as what Edward Soja, following Henri Lefebvre, called the "thirdspace," a category that is neither the material space that we experience nor a representation of space.[8] Thirdspace is instead a space of representation, a space bearing the possibility of new meanings, a space activated through social action and the social imagination. Multiple public activities are currently transforming Los Angeles everyday spaces, among them the garage sale and street vending.

8
Edward Soja,
THIRDSPACE: JOUR-
NEYS TO LOS ANGELES
AND OTHER REAL AND
IMAGINED PLACES
(New York: Basil
Blackwell, 1996).

THE GARAGE SALE

An unexpected outcome of the recession of the 1980s and the collapse of the real-estate market in Southern California was the proliferation of garage sales, even in the city's wealthiest areas. As an increasing number of people found themselves un- or underemployed, the struggle for supplemental income turned garage sales into semipermanent events, especially on the west side of Los Angeles. Cities such as Beverly Hills have passed ordinances limiting the number of garage sales per household to two per year. The front yard, an already ambiguous territory, serves as a buffer between residential privacy and the public street. Primarily an honorific space, the lawn is activated as the garage sale turns the house inside out, displaying the interior on the exterior. Presenting worn-out possessions, recently the contents of closets and drawers, for public viewing and purchase transforms the usually empty lawn into a site of representation. Unwanted furniture, knickknacks, and clothes are suddenly accessible to anyone passing by, melding the public and the extremely private. The same economic forces that caused the proliferation of garage sales also produced their mobile clientele, shoppers who drive through the city in search of sales or who discover them accidentally on the way to somewhere else.

In the Mexican American barrio East Los Angeles, with its less affluent population of homeowners and low real-estate values, commerce and domesticity have coexisted for a long time. A more permanent physical restructuring has already taken place, generated by a distinct set of social and economic needs: the front yard is marked by a fence, delineating an enclosure. The fence structures a more complex relationship between home and street. Different configurations of house, yard, and fence offer flexible spaces that can easily be adapted for commercial purposes. The fence itself becomes a display for ads or goods. Paving the lawn, a widespread practice, creates an outdoor shop. For Latino women who don't work outside the house, the garage sale has become a permanent business. Many move beyond recycling used items to buying and reselling clothes from nearby garment factories. Garages are simultaneously closets and shops, further linking the commercial and the domestic and producing a public place for neighborhood women. Men use the paved yards differently, as spaces for auto repair or car customizing. This attracts other neighborhood men, establishing a gathering place that is similarly domestic and commercial.

STREET VENDORS

All over the city, informal vendors appropriate marginal and overlooked sites chosen for their accessibility to passing motorists and pedestrians: street corners, sidewalks, and parking lots and vacant lots that are often surrounded by chain-link fences. Through the types of goods they sell, vendors bring to these urban spaces the qualities of domestic life. Used dresses from innumerable closets form a mural of female identity. Cheap rugs cover the harshness of chain link, overlaying the fence with the soft textures and bright patterns of the interior, defining a collective urban living room and evoking a multiplicity of dwelling places, an analogue for the diversity of the city. The delicate patterning of lace, flowers, and pillows, the softness of T-shirts and stuffed animals—all invoke the intimacy of the interior rather than the no-man's-land of the street. In public places, familiar items such as tables, chairs, and tablecloths, usually seen inside the home, transform neglected and underused space into islands of human occupation. Exchange both commercial and social, including that of the messages transmitted by T-shirts and posters, takes place. The vendors' temporary use hijacks these spaces, changing their meaning. Publicly owned spaces are briefly inhabited by citizens; private spaces undergo an ephemeral decommodification. Temporarily removed from the marketplace, these spaces now represent more than potential real-estate value.

Left and below: Garage sale in Mid-City

Orange seller's wares on median, Venice Boulevard

Vending display at curbside, La Brea Avenue, Baldwin Hills

Chain-link display, Sixth Street, MacArthur Park

Vendor, La Brea Avenue, Baldwin Hills

Driveway/commercial space, East Los Angeles

Vendor, Alvarado Street

Vending is a complex and diverse economy of microcommerce, recycling, and household production. Like the garage sale, vending supplements income rather than constituting an occupation—or, more likely, supports only the most marginal of existences. The varieties of vending visible across the city publicly articulate its multiple economic and social narratives. In neighborhoods populated by Central American immigrants, women prepare or package food or craft items in the home for sale on the sidewalk, extending the domestic economy into urban space. The social dramas of migration to Los Angeles are played out daily on the streets. The ubiquitous orange sellers, found on street dividers all over the city, are recent and undocumented arrivals who work to pay off the *coyote* who brought them across the border. Other immigrants vend for economic mobility, an alternative to sweatshop labor, that may eventually lead to a stall at a swap meet or to a small shop. Both sellers and goods can be read as local messages, attesting to the economic necessities and cultural values of a neighborhood.

Vending on public property, streets, and sidewalks is illegal in both the city and county of Los Angeles. When enough vendors congregate in a single place regularly enough, how-ever, they can muster the political power to change the nature of urban space. Chanting "We are vendors, not criminals," Central American vendors demonstrated at the Rampart police station, demanding the right to pursue their economic activities without police harassment. Since many of the vendors are undocumented, this makes them doubly illegal. Central American vendors have organized themselves, acquired legal representation, and pressured the city to change its laws to permit limited vending. Through the defense of their livelihood, vendors are becoming a political and economic force in the city.

DEMOCRACY AND PUBLIC SPACE

This brings us back to the question that started this investigation: how can public space be connected with democracy? Individual garage sales might not in themselves generate a new urban politics, but the juxtapositions, combinations, and collisions of people, places, and activities that I've described create a new condition of social fluidity that begins to break down the separate, specialized, and hierarchical structures of everyday life in Los Angeles. Local yet also directed to anyone driving or passing by, these unexpected intersections may possess the liberatory potential that Henri Lefebvre attributes to urban life. As chance encounters multiply and proliferate, activities of everyday space may begin to dissolve some of the predictable boundaries of race and class, revealing previously hidden social possibilities that suggest how the trivial and marginal might be transformed into a kind of micropolitics.

In some specific circumstances, as I've suggested, the intersection of publics, spaces, and identities can begin to delineate a new urban arena for democratic action that challenges normative definitions of how democracy works. Specifically constituted counterpublics organized around a site or activity create what anthropologist James Holston calls "spaces of insurgent citizenship."[9] These emergent sites accompany the changes that are transforming cities such as Los Angeles. Global and local processes, migration, industrial restructuring, and other economic shifts produce social reterritorialization at all levels. Residents with new histories, cultures, and demands appear in the city and disrupt the given categories of social life and urban space. Expressed through the specific needs of everyday life, their urban experiences increasingly become the focus of their struggle to redefine the conditions belonging to society. Once mobilized, social identities become political demands, spaces and sites for political transformation, with the potential to reshape cities.

The public sites where these struggles occur serve as evidence of an emerging but not yet fully comprehensible spatial and political order. In everyday space, differences between the domestic and the economic, the private and the public, and the economic and the political are blurring. Rather than constituting the failure of public space, change, multiplicity, and contestation may in fact constitute its very nature. In Los Angeles, the materialization of these new public spaces and activities, shaped by lived experience rather than built space, raises complex political questions about the meaning of economic participation and citizenship. By recognizing these struggles as the germ of an alternative development of democracy, we can begin to frame a new discourse of public space, one no longer preoccupied with loss but instead filled with possibility.

9
James Holston, "Spaces of Insurgent Citizenship," PLANNING THEORY 13 (summer 1996): 30-50.

THE URBAN BRICOLEUR

Mona Houghton

Ernest's Garden
Photographs by Dennis Keeley

For years I have walked the trails and footpaths of Laurel Canyon, and in my hiking I have grown to know the people who live in these hills. Many are like me—hippies who moved here in their twenties and are now well into middle age. The older people, though (the ones over seventy), are my favorites, for they are a breed unto their own. And there are a lot of them. They've been here for years and years, as many as fifty years in some instances. What makes them unique as an older group is that all of them are real bohemians, more bohemian than their forty- or fifty-something counterparts. They must be, because, in the mid-1960s and early 1970s, any forty-year-old who wasn't inherently eccentric fled. The man who lived in the house I now occupy up and moved when the band Iron Butterfly moved in across the street. "That," said my predecessor, "was the last straw." But before and during those summers of love, there *was* a settled community here that found the influx of dope-smoking, long-haired panhandlers a refreshing change. And so they stayed.

There is one particular man in this group whose company I regularly seek out, Ernest Rosenthal. I first met Ernest fourteen years ago. My dog, a puppy then, demanded an extraordinary amount of exercise, and in an effort to tire her I wandered farther and farther down the dirt roads, letting the four-legged lunatic cover ten miles to my every one. Late one afternoon I decided to push it, to continue even further, Chaco racing before me. And so I rounded the sharp curve. Before me I saw more hillside covered in chaparral, and a barn-red house out on a promontory with its bay window overlooking Kirkwood Canyon. Then the road narrowed and disappeared into a dark tunnel of arching eucalyptus trees, unkempt, ragged, and rangy. I was curious and kept going.

Chaco, ahead of me by two hundred feet, darted into the shadowy cave only to scramble back into the daylight moments later, eyebrows drawn. My steps slowed. Cautiously I moved into this netherworld.

As my eyes slowly adjusted to the darkness I saw above me huge yellow flowers entwined with the eucalyptus branches. Copa di oro, last week's buds, shriveled and rotting, pungent and sweet, dying and blooming, covered the ground before me. Goose bumps multiplied down the sides of my body as I continued on.

To my left I saw a driveway going up to a house that must have been on the bluff beyond. To my right, through thick foliage held at bay by disparate sections of fence (picket, grape stake, dog-eared), I could barely make out a clearing of sorts, with traces of narrow paths, some ceramic pots hanging from tree branches, a trellis perhaps? Intrigued, I reached out, spread some branches, and tried to see more.

"Excuse me?"

I jumped and turned. Before me stood a small, wiry man with thinning gray hair brushed up and away from his face, a gray beard drawn precisely along his jawline, carefully trimmed and well kept. He had a *real* nose, one with character and size, and blue eyes that did not leave my face. His tattered clothes hugged his compact and tight body—a strong chest, arms delineated by muscle. He had a kerchief tied around his neck, and on his feet were boots, each laced shut with a length of wire.

"Oh, hi," I said, embarrassed and feeling like a snoop.

"Can I help you?"

I pointed to the wall of bushes. "It's beautiful down there."

"It's spring," he replied.

Chaco, seeing a squirrel dart down a tree, grazed the man's knee as she dashed forward. After apologizing, I started off after my dog.

"My name is Ernest Rosenthal," he said to my back.

I turned and told him my name.

That night my dog slept the whole night through without once waking me up and so the new walk became a favorite one. It must have been on my third or fourth trip into the shadows before I again ran into Ernest. This time he was digging away at the earth near the roadway, using a handy, well-worn, short-handled pick he called a piton, a tool used in rock climbing. It would be years before I heard about his youth in Austria, between the world wars when he had climbed in the Alps. On this particular day, Ernest did not have time to linger. He needed to prepare the earth for an Australian tree fern he'd found along the roadside. It must have blown out of a pickup truck, he said, before focusing back on his task.

I kept taking that same walk. With each passing I became more familiar with the lay of the land near Ernest's place. It seemed that his property spanned both flanks of a hill, one side towering over Kirkwood Canyon and the other over Laurel Canyon. From a certain vantage point I could glimpse the roof of the house, small and snuggled in against the hill.

One Friday afternoon, Ernest popped out of the bushes as Chaco and I passed by.

"My wisteria is blooming," he said, and then he invited me into the garden to see. After slipping a leash on the unaccommodating Chaco and tying her to a post, I followed Ernest through the gate.

He started down a narrow set of stairs and I stumbled after him, trying hard to keep up with this man who must have been more than twice my age, and certainly half my size. He paused on a landing and I came to a stop at his side. The rich smell of dirt filled the cool, clear air. I felt Ernest watching me as I took it in—the house to my right, all rough-hewn wood and glass, and before me an oasis, lush with greens of every hue, trees, vines, and shrubs. From the road I had only seen the canopy.

"The wisteria is over here," he said, scampering off and down to the left.

I took in as much as I could while at the same time careening after my host, fearing that if I broke visual contact with him I would be forever lost in a maze of intersecting paths and stairways. Everything I saw folded back in on itself, grew up and back down, creating a sense of one continuous piece, although in reality what wasn't flora was an odd assortment of metal, stones, and wood: tire rims, car ramps, rebar, galvanized pipe, sheet metal, milk crates, brick, cement blocks, boulders, chipboard, and masonite, all seeming actually to rise

from the ground, as much a part of the landscape as the blue gums and citriodoras, the golden bamboo, and the acacias (purple leaf, mescat, and pearl).

Ernest disappeared around a bend. I sped up my pace but stopped when my eyes found him again. He was standing in a small clearing, head back, youthful in his tan leggings and tight, dark green T-shirt, both of which looked like he had snagged them out of the children's bin at the Goodwill. But his face is what really caught me, angel-like wonder, reveling in the satisfaction of what is, a connection made. Ernest was peering up at a skyful of blooming wisteria, stems heavy, bunches of blue hanging down from an arbor, fat bumblebees diving in.

Since that first evening under the wisteria, Ernest and I have been friends. I take anyone I know who's willing to walk as far as Ernest's gate and ask Ernest if he has the time to share his delight. He always does. Often when I walk by in the evening, Chaco no longer running ahead but now at my side, her graying muzzle held high in the breeze, Ernest will invite me in to see something special, perhaps an addition to his labyrinth (more terraced hillside thanks to some cast-off railroad ties he's found) or a particularly beautiful plant. Earnest always has something new, something blooming, or a spectacular creation. (This year it was a huge aviarylike structure—chicken wire stretched over vast rebar arches and held in place with wire brackets, stuck into six five-yard-long cement-footed lengths of galvanized pipe two inches in diameter. In this outdoor dome Earnest grows vegetables, bounty now safe from the deer, raccoons, and possums, from the scrub jays and mockingbirds.)

Over the years I have spotted Ernest here and there loading the bed of his minitruck with discarded materials. He isn't particular about his found stuff—anything from old roof rafters to scrap metal of every sort, body parts from cars, refrigerators, washing machines, barbecues. He picks up anything that might possibly be used to shape and maintain the two steep hillsides that reflect his vision—a magical other place where he, and anyone who visits, can lose themselves, can give themselves over to the marvel of it all.

But what attracts me to Ernest the most, more than any one event or action, is what I learn from the experience of him. Ernest stays engaged. In the twenty years since he retired from teaching at a state university, Ernest has unleashed his imagination on a mountaintop. He has the spirit every day to step outside his back door and find within himself a landscape that demands expression.

Last week I happened upon Ernest on the northeast corner of his property, his kerchief tied around his now bald pate. He was installing an elaborate wrought-iron gate. He found it, he told me, in a dumpster outside a house that was being remodeled. Despite the fact that it would open onto nothing, onto a steep and disappearing hillside I told him how beautiful I thought the gate was. He agreed.

"And after the cement dries," he continued, "once it's in place, I'll have to make something worthy of it out here." He waved his piton into the void. He laughed and pulled a battered level from the pocket of his oversized gangbanger denim shorts.

I left him holding the level against the vertical upright, knowing that in a month or two or three, I will pass by this same spot and now be invited to follow my friend down a set of stairs made from, perhaps, lengths of car ramp or logs from a fallen eucalyptus tree. These stairs will lead to a path or two, wandering through a patch of Canary Island broom and basket of gold, or cornflowers and blue marguerites.

Ernest participates. He surrounds himself in this project that knows no end, where there is always room for him to express himself. Here there is no boundary, because Ernest is the urban bricoleur.

A CURMUDGEON'S GUIDE TO THE WIDE WORLD OF TRASH

John Chase

Where there's trash, there's life. One weekend I arrived at the offices I share with friends to find that a sociopathic therapist had made a major deposit in our dumpster. It was all too easy to reconstruct the trail of sorrow this man had wrought. Among his psychojunk were angry letters from the female clients he'd romanced and slept with. You could see why they'd be especially vengeful from the other supporting evidence left behind. There was a huge, almost competent watercolor of a new-age angel looking benevolent and radiating healing and forgiveness. For all I know, this dumpster therapist had an assortment of stuffed animals and Winnie the Pooh bears for his patients to hug as they were lulled into a spurious sense of safety and caring.

This simultaneously healing and wounding shrink had also left behind all of the most dubious and pat self-help books—babbling tomes on putting the sexual magic back into your marriage, manuals detailing how many scoops of ice cream to give to your inner child. Part of me felt that a call to the state licensing board was in order. Another part of me said that this particular therapist was a veritable Chernobyl of bad karma and I did not want so much as one scintilla of it rubbing off on me. It seemed wiser to let the rubbish be hauled off to the bucolic oak tree–studded canyon at the edge of the San Fernando Valley that our waste-disposal firm is despoiling by filling with trash. At any rate, I'm sure that one of the many outraged women (that was the shocking thing—this was not just letters from one or two patients, but letters from many, many patients) had taken matters into her own hands. Hopefully Mr. Wonderful is now selling shoes or peddling insurance in another state, and

THE TWO CONQUERING VEHICLES OF ALLEYDOM:
THE DUMPSTER & THE SHOPPING CART.

no longer passing out Love Joneses like party favors. In any case, at least he's made one contribution to society by proving my point: trash is indeed a supple medium for the recording of human behavior.

Since nearly all possessions ultimately end up as garbage, the trash universe as a topic is virtually infinite. Rather than take on the whole dumpster, so to speak, I will instead confine my remarks to trash as geographical marker, trash as barter and livelihood, and trash as symbol. These are my trash territories of choice.

It's natural for anyone who lives, as I do, on an alley in the seaside Los Angeles neighborhood of Venice to be obsessed with trash. The alleys of Venice are twenty-four-hour open-air markets for the depositing, sorting, trading, redeeming, and removing of refuse. These transactions are created in part by legislation designed to encourage recycling. Cans, bottles, and paper products bring cash when redeemed—not very much cash, but just enough to make the collection worthwhile to the homeless and the poor. They know that the alleys of Venice are paved with soda bottles and cardboard. These trash-for-cash transactions are supplemented by area residents' trash-can-top charitable donations of old clothing and other cast-offs.

Trash is disorder personified, the horrifying proof that wanted possessions are all potential changelings, that even the most benign activities have a fecal underworld. The lush landscape becomes lawn clippings, a feast becomes bones, the cupidlike infant produces soiled Pampers. To control trash is to strike a symbolic blow at entropy. I learned this early in life from my parents. From my mother I learned that matching candlesticks and place settings conquered all. In order not to offend the Goddess of Propriety, social offerings were to be piled on the altar of hospitality just so.

From my father I learned the watchful art of disposing the remains of these offerings as well as the finer points of trash management. Pop selected his pleasures and his worries carefully. Both categories were geared toward direct action, whether in the purchase and consumption of pickled pigs' feet or in rising early to meet the garbagemen. The trashmen as I understood them in my youth were one of the armies of service workers who swarmed to upper-middle-class suburbs in Southern California to renew the gloss on utopia, ensuring that floors shone, that beds had fresh linen, or that sprinkler heads gave off the correct fine spray. As a child I hated the fact that Pop would even question the inevitability and completeness of these arrangements, provisions I was eager to take for granted as base conditions for existence. If the trash scenario looked dicey to Pop, if he knew full well in his stewardship of 1410 Milan Avenue that our weekly garbage output exceeded either the legal or social conditions for removal, he would spend days in advance fretting and plotting strategy. This strategy usually involved my father materializing at just the right moment with the proper amount of folded green for the garbagemen.

At the end of his life this concern with order increased. I arrived at my father's house at various times to find it awash in tangled paper trails, decades of bills, tax returns, and personal documents, residue that covered the living room in the same way that pictures of my sister and myself at all ages had once overrun the living room, laid out by my mother during an uncontrollable manic-depressive high.

Control the trash, control the universe. Control all the air escaping from the heavens of meaning and utility into the larger formless, shapeless, and hostile cosmos. My father's obsession with the choreography of trash removal annoyed me to no end. It clearly was not a fit subject of concern for a grown man. Naturally that meant I would soon find myself just as compulsive in that arena as he, if not more so. At some point in my thirties, I contracted his nervous tic of kicking crumpled cigarette wrappers and crushed beer cans into the gutter. It now takes a certain amount of willpower for me to walk past a tempting pile of crumpled cigarette packs and not give them a good swift boot. I am embarrassed to realize that, in some primitive part of my brain, I somehow think I am making the world a better place with my carefully aimed punt.

My real introduction to the tidal and seasonal flows of the trash world occurred when I lived on Sanborn Street in Silverlake, another Los Angeles neighborhood, where a new deposit of flotsam and jetsam would wash up daily from the flow of auto and pedestrian traffic. One day it would be the endless ticker-tape strands of broken audiocassettes, the next I would find the unwanted portions of multiple McDonald's Happy Meals. Each bright dawn brought with it a virgin sunrise, a fresh edition of the morning paper, and a new load of bottles, cans, and candy wrappers. Unless I went out there every day to litterpick, the front yard always ended up looking like Woodstock the morning after.

When I moved to Venice I was no longer the King of Trash. On my new block that title clearly belongs to Butch, a white-bearded cynic with most, but not all, of the teeth he was born with. Butch rules the roost as manager of the building next door. I refer to Butch's building as Tenement 911 due to the violently colorful behavior of its inhabitants. Over the two years I have had a good view of Tenement 911's dumpster, I have watched Butch finesse the trash to a fare-thee-well. Butch is not above climbing into the bin and jumping up and down to squash the trash so the lid will close.

TENEMENT 911 REAR DOOR VIGNETTE
AFTER A DECEMBER RAIN.

Butch has kept a particularly vigilant eye on the dumpster's contents ever since a local fish restaurant began sneaking their reeking offal into the container. I could sympathize because a dental lab down the street from a building where I once had my office used to fill our dumpster with bloody cotton swabs and plaster denture molds in the dead of night. Nothing short of a padlock will stop a lawless dumpster dumper. I didn't like this dental dumpster concept, because I was always absent-mindedly throwing away important items, and then having to jump into the dumpster and fish around for the lost item in question.

Twice a day when Butch takes his supervisorial constitutional around the block with his wife's Chihuahua the lid is lifted and the contents inspected for suspect, nontenement debris. Woe betide he or she who steals space in that dumpster. Butch's dumpster-management policy consists of immediately returning the foreign items to their presumed owner (I know from personal experience that he doesn't always guess correctly) as well as ferreting out any potential items of value for himself or his tenants. There are times when Butch himself nabs the recyclables; whether he sorts out the bottles and cans to supplement his beer fund or to prevent alley prowlers from profiting is something I have not as yet established.

The city of Los Angeles has instituted an elaborate, officially sanctioned recycling program, complete with specially engineered but nonetheless temperamental garbage trucks that occasionally come apart and kill hapless motorists, garbage cans to fit the trucks, and little plastic recycling bins for the more precious cargo of metal and glass. Each of the garbage cans is individually numbered, a marvel of obsessional bureaucratic thinking. Crack may be sold with impunity on the streets of Los Angeles, and vast disparities exist in educational, social, and professional opportunity and between different neighborhoods and demographic and ethnic groups. Yet somewhere the bureaucratic geniuses who came up with this brazenly utopian plan of action are counting their numbered trash receptacles as the cans are flung into the trucks—like sheep jumping a rail—as they settle into a deep slumber, happy that Angelenos now live in a city with orderly refuse.

The centralized issue of pedigreed trash cans seems, in a sense, entirely un-American. It feels as if Los Angelenos can't be trusted with their personal and household hygiene, and perhaps the next step is officially dispensed toilet brushes, dental floss, and clean under-wear. And, as with many new government programs, the remedy for one problem sows the seeds for another. By requiring that the trash cans and recycling bins be placed in the street, the trashnocrats have eliminated tens of thousands of parking spaces at one fell swoop. They have altered the delicate parking ecosystem in neighborhoods across the city, without giving the slightest thought as to where the displaced cars might go.

The regimented rows of regulation-issue cans lack the sangfroid of their traditional metal predecessors. It is difficult to imagine alley cats yowling at the full moon atop these modern-age neophytes. The new cans would be equally unimpressive when hurled aside by a getaway car in a high-speed chase scene. Neither do they bear marks of age with the graceful distinction of their dentable, rustable forerunners. Basically, if you've seen one official city of Los Angeles trash can, you've seen them all.

In real life, much of this elaborate civic infrastructure is simply ignored. Recycling in Venice is not done by the city, because there is nothing left to recycle by the time the city trucks arrive: the bright yellow plastic bins have already been scoured clean by squadrons of can, paper, and bottle pickers. The recycling program is a metaphor for the ways in which government officials and the vocal public increasingly attempt to legislate a perfect world that will not harm anyone in any conceivable way under any conceivable scenario. It is a perfection so demanding of ordinary citizens in the pursuit of ordinary tasks that the overtaxed masses just begin to ignore the perfect rules altogether. Thus the theoretical bureaucratic world of trash recycling and the barter economy of discarded goods coexist side by side.

It is a neighborhood that champions the eccentric and the dispossessed. The alley becomes for me an internalized zone of contention between my own enjoyment of the iconoclastic Venice milieu and my bourgeois desires for predictability, familiarity, and physical separation from the damaged and the dispossessed.

The trash of Venice is a medium of exchange between income groups that acts as a privatized and informal form of welfare. Someone who has decided that the time has come to part ways with a garment will, more often than not, lay it gently on top of a trash container, or perhaps even display it enticingly, clean, folded, and pressed. Once upon a time this cast-off clothing might have been ferried to a thrift store. My neighbor believes that she is being a Good Samaritan when she places these offerings on my trash can. To me, this charitable placement is a breach of my territorial rights and a subsidy to the alternative alley economy that I do not appreciate. Hurling her offerings into the depths of my garbage always gives me a momentary surge of illusory control. Despite this pique over the sovereignty of my trash cans I have been known to play Lord Bountiful myself. Particularly when I was first moving in, and sorting through the possessions I had recently inherited, it was tempting to leave rejected articles in the alley.

I am ambivalent about this laissez-faire system because some of the scavengers in my

TWILIGHT STEALS OVER THE HALF-EMPTY
PUMP DISPENSER OF LUBRI-DERM AND
RUNNING SHOES, PLACED ATOP MY TRASH
CAN (REGULATION L.A. CITY ISSUE) BY
MY NEIGHBOR WHO BELIEVES CHARITY
BEGINS AT <u>MY</u> HOME. THE SMOKE
TRAILS FROM THE VENT ARE VAPOR
FROM MY DRYER.

AS THE SUN SETS OVER THE PACIFIC
JUST BELOW THE PALM TREE
A CHEERFUL, WHISTLING ALLEYITE
RUMMAGES THROUGH A DUMPSTER.

alley are primarily alcoholics and drug addicts. The emaciated, bearded old man who beds down in the open garage across from mine often goes to sleep with the needle still sticking out of his arm. That's not something I would willingly choose to live near, nor is it behavior to which I would contribute any kind of de facto financial support.

In the space of the alley, mediation between economic castes and between legal and illegal activities occurs. When a housed alley resident neatly lines up a row of empty bottles against a wall, or carefully folds a newly laundered but worn blanket on top rather than inside a garbage can, that person becomes part of a transaction in which something that no longer has value to one economic class becomes valuable to another economic class. The excess and unwanted remnants of the housed alleyites' existence become the lifeblood of the nomadic alleyites. Trash becomes the medium of exchange; residents get swift removal of unwanted goods, supplemented by the psychic rewards of charity. By the time the discards sit on the alley they have ceased to have economic value as a commodity to their owners. Placing them in the alley restores a fraction of their original value, because they are now the stock in trade of the unofficial economy.

From time to time, I witness attempts to find new uses for the found objects. One midwinter day at dusk, I arrived home to find an alley gypsy intently refashioning a large periwinkle ceramic vase. He was pounding the vessel on the pavement, methodically knocking fragments off its lip. As he worked, he periodically stopped to hold up the vase and appraise his progress. When he had finished removing the bulk of the lip, he began to rotate the vase on the ground in an effort to grind off its vestigial remains. He must have deemed the final product a failure, for he left it sitting there, in the parking lot of Tenement 911, where today it still sits.

The deposit of trash is a territorial matter. If a person leaves trash somewhere, he or she lays claim to that spot in the same way that an animal does by leaving its scent along a trail. If someone throws a bottle over my fence after polishing off the last sip, a claim has been made on my yard. When there are enough wrappers, newspapers, and other detritus swirling around my small patch of land, I feel I have lost control of my territory. At one point, when Tenement 911 harbored its party-heartiest crew, there was much difference between the trash crop I confronted in Silverlake and the harvest I found on my doorstep at the beach.

Trash is a visible record of alley occupation, and activity level, present and future—the amount of garbage-can pilfering and strewn trash reflects the alley's current homeless population, while the presence or absence of large amounts of trash indicates the social order that will prevail in the near future. The moments when the alley most looks like a cross between the *Road Warrior* and *Repo Man* sets, adrift in overturned cans and overflowing shopping carts, are precisely the moments when the gypsy contingent grows largest and most active. Like sea gulls trailing a fishing ship, the garbage sorters fill the alley in greatest numbers just before the city trucks arrive on Tuesday morning because that is when the pickings are most abundant.

Along the alley, house and yard are recognized by all as clearly defined zones of private domesticity. The placement of no-longer-wanted items in the alley transforms their off-limits, owned status; the goods are now fair game for the public at large. As the prey of nomads, these floating possessions mark the boundaries of public and private space. The edges of private space along the alley are defined by small architectural elements—a set of two or three steps, a stub of half-height wall, or an overhanging balcony. An unlocked yard with no trash cans is likely to remain untouched by outsiders for years at a time, even if it holds relatively transportable items of some minimal value, such as a child's tricycle, because they cannot be easily converted into ready cash. Put a trash can in that yard and the equation changes; it is suddenly far more likely that itinerant alleyites will feel compelled to violate the private space out of the need to sift the can's contents for recyclable booty. The presence of trash defines any space as an adjunct part of the alley, converting it into de facto public space. At the high-water mark right before garbage pickup, the public space of the alley extends to the parking lot of Tenement 911 next door.

Tonight at seven o'clock, four bedrolls will appear in the open garage twenty-five feet from my house. The people who sleep on them are probably the fifth or sixth generation to house themselves in that garage since I moved here two years ago. The alley has a human ecology of its own, and any sense of residential vacuum is quickly filled. The current denizens of the garage happen to be meticulous in their inhabitation. They arrive and depart at set hours. They have no shopping carts, they do not leave large piles of possessions behind when they are not around, and they do not invite large crowds of hangers-on. For all practical purposes, the garage might as well be a hotel room with a printed set of rules and a check-out time posted on the door. These prudent lodgers limit signs of their occupation and curtail their transgressions of the nominally private space so as not to jeopardize their tenuous right to continued nocturnal occupation.

The alley functions as public space in the truest sense of the word—no one is excluded. The homeless people who sleep in the garage opposite my house are just as much residents of the alley, for whatever time they remain there, as I am, because on those

SCRATCHING POST, RECYLING BIN
(AS YET UNPLUNDERED) AND WOOD BUNNY
BY BACK STEPS. (THERE USED TO BE 2
BUNNIES BUT SOMEONE STOLE THE OTHER
BROTHER BUNNY)

CAST YOUR BREAD UPON THE ASPHALT:
WONDER NO MORE:
RATHER PIGEON FEED

nights they are no more unclear about where they sleep or what space they inhabit than I. During prime daylight hours, the alley falls under the purview of beachgoers taking a short-cut. This use of space is also determined by the weather: the hotter and sunnier the day, the greater the numbers of surf-seekers. At still other times, the janitorial staff of the "Zona Rosa" apartment building takes possession of the area and runs a bootleg appliance-repair business in a closed garage next to the open garage where the homeless sleep. During some periods, the alley is actually dominated by the rent-paying tenants of the other apartment house across the alley from me (the non–Tenement 911 building), who, to my astonishment, defy the inhospitable alley environment by actually using their balconies to water their plants and talk on the phone outdoors.

Because the alley space is not officially defined or regulated, illegal activities inevitably occur therein. Sometimes the alley is used as a latrine, sometimes not. There are ebbs and flows of public drug use. During the tail end of one wild period at Tenement 911, the alley functioned as a kind of annex to the building. I would bound down the steps of my house to find a virtual convention of shopping carts. A selection of purloined and salvaged wares would be laid out in front of my garage door and surrounded by a crowd of appraising alleyites, the scavenging equivalent of a gaggle of suburban shoppers comparing notes at a yard sale. There have also been instances of theft in the alley, especially of bicycles or tools from workmen's trucks. The asphalt in the alley is often dusted with the residue of break-ins, the emerald crumbs of shattered car windows.

The two categories of alleyites, nomadic and residential, are not mutually exclusive, nor is it always possible to classify someone as belonging exclusively to one group over the other. There are also various fleeting networks of association among alley-facing residents, networks that sometimes entwine the vagabonds. Tenement 911 has housed rent-paying people who were friends with some of the roving alleyites. Sometimes the apartment dwellers caroused with the gypsies in the alley, and other times the gypsies slept with the apartment dwellers in their abodes. The reformed speed freak in the apartment house across the way and the former cocaine dealer who lives adjacent to the alley (the former charming, the latter not) shared a friend in common who slept either in the cocaine dealer's car or in the former speed freak's apartment. Muttering and sputtering, he was often to be found working on his battered truck, which was pieced together with rope and cardboard. His most frequent method of entry to the vehicle entailed crawling over the permanently lashed together and therefore useless driver's-side door.

The tiny cottage at the corner of the alley, vacant for years, was taken over by a former

I STRONGLY SUSPECT MY EVIL NEIGHBOR TWO
DOORS DOWN OF ABANDONING HIS SKELETAL
CHRISTMAS TREE IN THE ALLEY JUST TO ANNOY
EVERYONE.

Tenement 911 dweller through a special deal he had arranged with the landlord. The house was filled with junk, so he solved the problem by dumping loads of the detritus in various locations. Piles of it would appear overnight in the public parking lot at the corner, in front of Tenement 911, and in my garbage cans, furtively stuffed when this borderline sociopath thought I wasn't looking.

Acquaintances the new cottager had made on the streets and in the alley appeared and disappeared as signaled by the alternate display and striking down of various curtains and bed sheets, semaphore for the presence or absence of a tryst in progress. In the crawl space beneath the house, a good four feet tall at best, pieces of paper installed as window dressings for the tiny wire-mesh screens marked the presence of visitors. A few days later, the pieces of paper would vanish and the lock would reappear on the dwarfish crawl-space door.

Prior to the Tenement 911 alumnus's tenancy, the house had been occupied by one of the alley gypsies, an infamous local drunk who bore pink and mottled scar tissue on his toes. The evil sot loved to hurl pornographic insults at women and scathing challenges to masculinity at men. Crafty and misanthropic, he slipped in and out under the cover of darkness, across the yard of my charitable neighbors. They knew full well that he was living there, but on principle would never dispossess anyone of their habitation.

The alley space is not really a static topography so much as it is an urban tidal zone in which those with less privilege and weaker legal or financial buttress for their residency float through more quickly than those who have more assurance in these matters. The alley exists in many other incarnations besides its guise as the space of trash. Nonetheless, trash is one of the forces that determines the character, and the use, of the place. At the same time the detritus acts as an ongoing record of local current events. Like other aspects of everyday urbanism, the study of trash reveals the interaction of both officially sanctioned and unsanctioned actions. As the accretion of many small acts by a series of individuals, the disposition of trash becomes a de facto user survey that explains why and how urban spaces are used, experienced, and valued.

634 Alvarado Street, MacArthur Park: December 1996

This Salvadoreño pointed to the architectural ornament over the arch and said, "That was then." Looking at the signs inside the arch, he said, "This is now."

THEY SAW A VERY GREAT FUTURE HERE: LOS ANGELES, LATINO METROPOLIS

Camilo José Vergara

Images that seek to dazzle through emphasis on people and dramatic lighting do not disclose urban forms. If allowed, buildings can direct the eye to a human story, one that will account for the appearance and function of the structure. I consider my work as a means through which cities can tell their recent history and look to urban residents as the main interpreters of their surroundings.

These pictures of Los Angeles were taken during 1996 and 1997. On five previous visits, I had photographed South Central, Skid Row, Compton, and East Los Angeles. I noticed differences in my later excursions that surprised me, and I tried to capture those differences in these photographs. In a city where the single-family house has predominated, for example, there are now many new multiple-occupancy dwellings more characteristic of older American metropolises; they are changing the look of Los Angeles neighborhoods. Los Angeles is famous for its murals, yet I found more vitality and spontaneity in commercial and religious signs.

As I roamed the city, I was struck by the extent of the transition in South Central and Compton from predominantly African American to predominantly Latino populations. I was not surprised when Esmeralda, a hairdresser, called the area around Twentieth Street and South Central Avenue "un Mejico chiquito" (a little Mexico). The abundance of "for sale" and "for rent" signs from Latino real-estate agents in front of houses indicated that better off African American families continue to move out of South Central. As African Americans become a minority in their neighborhood, tension is created, arising from both real and symbolic assertions of territoriality.

From opposite perspectives, a black engineer and a Latino worker both commented on the influx of Spanish-speaking people to Southeast Los Angeles by saying: "They came to create their own Mexico." What the Latino saw was the return to a land that once belonged to them, a cause for rejoicing. What the black man saw was an "invasion" that was lowering wages and bringing smelly, second-rate stores to the community. He repeated several times, "They multiply."

In New York, I showed some of my Los Angeles work to audiences of urban specialists. Invariably they concluded that Los Angeles is a special urban case and things seem much better out West. This surprised me. Even Skid Row, with its missions, flophouses, small industries, and warehouses, was perceived as tremendously successful in generating jobs. These Eastern specialists encouraged me to look beyond the homeless in the foreground of my pictures to the industrial buildings behind them. Small-scale, interdependent businesses that make valued products, they represent a real urban economy.

"Little Mexico" is big and will grow much bigger. In Los Angeles County, Spanish-speaking people are surprised to find themselves in a Latino environment the size of Philadelphia, a situation unique in the history of immigration. They cannot understand why, in less than two decades, Anglos "moved to the mountains" and blacks retreated to the suburbs, leaving behind them such a large territory. Los Angeles is a surprise. In the poorest sections of this city's southeast, I witnessed how, without armor and horses, these present-day Conquistadores find themselves building a new world.

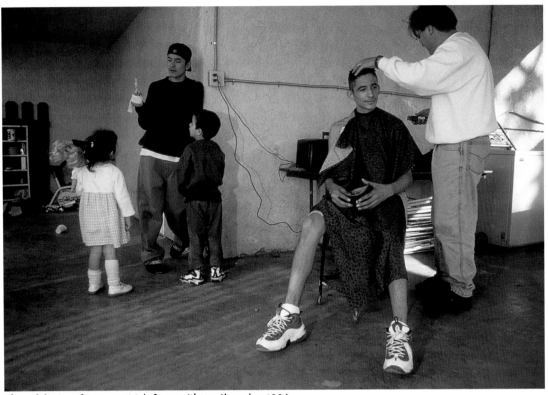

West of Juniper Street at 108th Street, Watts: November 1996

Juan the Barber makes house calls and also teaches young girls to waltz for their *quinceanera* parties. In the garage of a Watts "dingbat," he gives a haircut to fifteen-year-old Marc, whose family comes from Nayarit, Mexico.

Vernon Street at Kansas Avenue, Watts: November 1996
Juan and his son, Tony, sell mattresses from a factory owned by Juan's father-in-law from the front yard of their house. The mattresses sell for about $120.

Stockwell Street at Aranbe Avenue, Compton: January 1997
During the 1992 riots, Mrs. Young had the entire contents of her Compton store looted.
Her family moved their home away from the store. They would also like to open a new
store in another place.

Figueroa Street and Fifty-first Street, South Central: October 1996

Ramon and Berta are from Mexico. They wait for the bus holding business cards in their hands. Once on the bus they show their artwork to the passengers and try to get commissions.

Holmes Avenue and Sixty-first Street, South Central: November 1997

This truck belongs to José and Jesus Sandoval. Bought for $100, it does not run.
They use it as a shoe repair shop.

Main Street, South Central: October 1996

Signs such as this are placed on the fences enclosing vacant lots in South Central
Los Angeles.

Crenshaw Boulevard and Florence Avenue, South Central: February 1997

Jade's signs are tied to fences throughout South Central Los Angeles. All of them are rectangular, use a similar color scheme, and incorporate the triangle and the face, yet no two are the same.

Martin Luther King Jr. Boulevard and Crenshaw Boulevard, South Central: November 1996

These signs are tied to the fence of a former Texaco gas station.

Broadway between Florence Avenue and Seventy-third Street, South Los Angeles: October 1996
In less than a decade, the businesses on this block changed from African American to Latino. For some the street is a "little Mexico." For others, the transformation of the block is a sign that "they are taking over."

South Los Angeles: October 1996

An African American couple started this outdoor restaurant as an expansion of their car wash. Then a Mexican vendor parked his truck at the site, paid the owners five hundred dollars a month, and turned the restaurant into a Mexican food stand. After a year he returned to Mexico, but the owners of the car wash, realizing it was a good business, decided to run the food stand themselves.

237 Broadway, Downtown Los Angeles: October 1996
At this storefront, weddings start at around $160.

8-0551
237
237
OTROS SERVICIOS
LLENAMOS FORMAS
DE INMIGRACION
LEGALES
CASAMOS a MENORES
MISOS
VIAJE
TAX

Seventy-sixth Place, Watts: November 1996

In the garage of his house, Melvin, originally from Ecuador, finishes chair frames made in Spain. He also makes tables, chests of drawers, and other pieces of furniture. For each chair that sells for $800, he receives $120.

Central Avenue and Forty-first Street, South Central: August 1996

This furniture store expanded into an open lot formerly occupied by an auto-detail shop.

Part 2

MAKING
the City

JOHN KALISKI

THE PRESENT CITY
AND
THE PRACTICE
OF
CITY DESIGN

> *The purpose of the plan is to look to
> the future as well as to the present,
> to plan with vision, but not be visionary.*
>
> —Report of the Planning Commission,
> Houston, 1929

While the city can be studied, mapped, diagrammed, and probed from many professional perspectives, there is no substitute for the actual experience of a place. Whether encountered by foot, public transit, or car, while sitting on a bench, listening and observing, or through participation, the present city is the taken-for-granted everyday that surrounds us. I see one such example during my daily commute when I pass an auto-body shop. The design is nothing special. A chain-link fence marks the lot's perimeter. During the day, an oil-spotted concrete parking area is filled with smashed cars awaiting reconstructive surgery. Behind this open space sits an unfinished cinderblock building with metal roll-up doors punctuated by acrylic slot windows. Above the garage doors, white letters hand-painted on a cerulean background brightly proclaim the business. Squeezed between a 7-Eleven convenience store and a used-car dealership, the location is not distinguished, traditionally civic, or classically beautiful.

Each evening at about six o'clock, after the auto-body activity has concluded and the wrecks have been moved into the garage, a street vendor opens for business, selling *carne asada* (roasted meat) in the shop's parking lot. Wired to the chain-link fence is a cardboard sign hand-lettered "Tacos," the only formal announcement of this adjunct enterprise. Despite this low profile, a surprising number of people somehow find this improvised drive-in, pull their cars in from the busy avenue, and enjoy a snack or meal. After dark, the flames of the grill sear the meat and highlight the faces of the customers. The smoky glow of a single bare bulb dangles from a makeshift canopy and casts a white aura. By nine o'clock, the lot has emptied, the vendor departed, and the chain-link gate is drawn across the entryway.

To most design professionals, places such as this auto-body shop and meat-grilling operation remain invisible, illegal, or ugly. Yet this one daily ritual, multiplied

Sidewalk vending, Los Angeles, 1997

a hundred thousand times over, is the everyday city. It possesses its own type of beauty, one that claims space, solves site and program constraints with smart—if sometimes temporary—solutions, aspires for a better present, and works within a framework of given conditions and histories. The accumulated evidence of this city is all around, and it tells a remarkable human story. It has an energy that architects, landscape architects, planners, and urban designers try repeatedly to capture. Unfortunately, despite substantial and varied professional efforts, only a pale simulation of this everyday vitality is usually achieved in planned practices and projects. Why is designing an actual city so elusive? How can design in general, and urban designers in particular, create practices that promote the life of this present city?

THE DILEMMA OF URBAN DESIGN AND THE EVERYDAY CITY

Since the late nineteenth century, architects have attempted to transform the delights of the city directly into the principles of urban design. Even as they are inspired by the mysteries, horrors, and multiplicities of the modern city to create new forms, the dominant design ideologies of the last hundred years continue to be construed as essentialistic architectural truths. Over and over again, experience demonstrates that this type of truth-seeking precludes the vitality of urban experience that inspired architecture in the first place. The tension between modern architecture's quest for the conceptually pure and the plurality of the modern city defines the fundamental dilemma of twentieth-century urban design.

Le Corbusier's 1935 Ville Radieuse, or the Radiant City, is a now-hackneyed but still valuable example of the disharmony between architectural ideology and everyday urbanism. In its desire for utopian order, this vision simply did away with the situational rhythm of the urban. For Le Corbusier, the city did not need sidewalks for browsing and encountering the parade of daily life. He also rejected streets that would accommodate a mixture of ground-level uses as well as places that combined living and working. Rigorous separation of uses, people, buildings, and nature was consistently pursued. Embracing the hygienic critique of urban density and seeking to improve the lives of working men and women, Le Corbusier promoted the destruction of the existing physical city and its attendant urban situations. On the surface, the Radiant City promised an idyll. In its reduction of the city to a Garden of Eden, it reproduced the reactionary situations against which social modernism rebelled by promulgating a clearly visible absolute order. With radiance, the problematic city of visible difference is replaced with an even more problematic urbanism of unrelenting hierarchy.

The Radiant City is symbolic of the early modern architect's urge to design an ordered and controlled urbanism as if it were a functional building. This approach was forthrightly challenged after World War II. In the early 1950s, Team X injected the values of the traditional pedestrian-oriented street into architectural debates. Disputing the tenets of the Congrès Internationaux d'Architecture Moderne (CIAM) as exemplified in the Athens Charter of 1933, Team X members noted the critical point that "The short narrow street of the slum succeeds where spacious redevelopment frequently fails."[1] Team X wanted to introduce a fresh "spirit of hope" into architecture and the design of the city by utilizing in their designs observations of daily routines and understandings of existing urban patterns.[2] Their renewed interest in the timeless rhythms of everyday urban life paralleled their growing fascination with regionalism, vernacular building techniques, and history,

subjects suppressed by the modernism of an older generation of architects. For Team X, however, architecture and urbanism remained a discipline of abstraction. While foreshadowing the complexities of postmodernism, the group remained committed throughout the 1950s to the modern movement's aesthetics of internationalism, creating at times an uncomfortable juxtaposition between the goal of conceptual humanism and the group's actual results.

The contemporaneous work of the Austrian American architect Victor Gruen explored themes similar to those articulated by Team X, albeit in the context of a capitalist and market-oriented setting—suburban America of the 1950s and 1960s. Gruen, like Team X, endeavored to introduce an updated vision of the urban street into architectural practice. He combined his ideas of the street with Sigfried Giedion's concept of "space-time," described in *Space, Time and Architecture* as change, mobility, and the

1
Quoted in Kenneth Frampton, MODERN ARCHITECTURE: A CRITICAL HISTORY (New York: Oxford University Press, 1980), 271.

2
Alison Smithson, ed., TEAM 10 MEETINGS: 1953–1984 (New York: Rizzoli, 1991), 9.

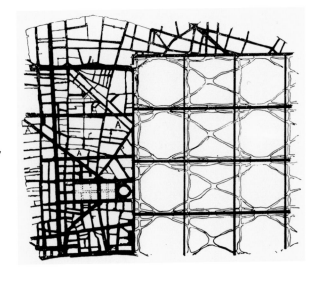

Le Corbusier, Ville Radieuse sketch, 1935

ability to conceptualize objects simultaneously from a variety of viewpoints.[3] These ideas influenced most modernists and are evident in Gruen's designs. Unlike Le Corbusier but similar to Team X, Gruen expanded the definition of simultaneity to embrace the urban social experience of the sidewalk. Gruen tried to re-create in his projects the complex relationship of daily patterns associated with storefronts, market squares, and contained plazas. He carefully studied these forms and their phenomena and used them as the basis for a new architecture of urbanism.

Gruen's greatest invention, the postwar American shopping mall, celebrated through space-time utility, efficiency, consumption, and the automobile. But Gruen also called upon his childhood memories of Vienna's rich urban life and attempted to endow his projects with the feeling of a social townscape. Proportion, dimension, and open space based on built precedent, as well as the inclusion of such civic amenities as post

offices, community rooms, and facilities for events—all were part of Gruen's concerted effort to will into being the activities and tenor of Main Street. Though Gruen pursued a traditional definition of civic life, albeit in diminished form, the shopping mall would develop in ways antithetical to the integrated town ideal that initially inspired him. From an analytical point of view, he noted the mall's "inability to absorb urban functions which are drawn to the immediate vicinity of centers into the physical context of the center itself."[4] From an empirical point of view, the shopping mall's commercial foundation coupled with its gigantism ultimately separated consumption from the desired program of daily life.

Within a context of financial exchange, shopping malls do nevertheless permit their own type of public display and difference. In this sense, Gruen's strategies linking modern architecture to the forms of traditional town life shifted architectural and urban design tactics even more profoundly

3
Sigfried Giedion, SPACE, TIME AND ARCHITECTURE (Cambridge, Mass.: Harvard University Press, 1941), 355-57.

4
Victor Gruen, CENTERS FOR THE URBAN ENVIRONMENT: SURVIVAL OF CITIES (New York: Van Nostrand Reinhold, 1973), 39.

Peter and Alison Smithson,
Berlin Hauptstadt project, 1957–58

than the work of Team X, which architecturally remained too abstract to achieve its desired effect. Building upon Gruen's influence, subsequent mall designers such as Benjamin Thompson, Jane Thompson, and Jon Jerde continue to attempt to manipulate the intractable mall formula and simulate town life. These efforts implicitly accept urban pluralism as the inspiration for urban design and architecture—they incorporate, for example, increasingly diverse activities and multilayered visual complexities, all intended to promote spontaneity—but they have invariably been constricted by the control mechanisms inherent in the mall. The experience of the shopping mall demonstrates that it is far from easy to overcome the gap between the design goal of urban spontaneity and the reality of social, economic, and political constraints. Whether form-oriented modernists rejecting the Athens Charter prescriptions or corporate architects working for market-driven developers, twentieth-century designers have found it nearly impossible to forge approaches that empower, rather than simulate, urban spontaneity.

The work of Team X and Victor Gruen anticipated the growing interest in the existing city and its continued relevance. This fascination with messy urbanism, contrasted with the modernist tendency to promote the rigorous separation of land uses, leads to an emphasis on the neighborhood as opposed to the house as the basic community building block, substitutes civic space for transportation systems, and replaces physical activity in open greenswards with

Gruen Associates, Winrock Center, Albuquerque, New Mexico 1961

broader definitions of space for recreation and leisure. The growing inclination in the 1950s and 1960s to equate good city design with a physical framework that would support social, rather than formal, simultaneity has constituted the core of urban design efforts and debates over the past forty years. The search for this framework and the quest to resolve its inherent contradictions continue to establish a primary intellectual context for contemporary architectural discourse.

In the United States, the most powerful popular critique of modern architecture's assault on the existing city was formed by Jane Jacobs, the godmother of American urban design. In *The Death and Life of Great American Cities* (1961) and *The Economy of Cities* (1969), she pointed to such traditional, organic elements as the city block, the coexistence of old and new buildings, fragmented parcelization, mixed uses, desirable congestion, and the efficiency of inefficiency as engendering a high quality of city life. Jacobs's celebrations of incremental, human-scale city construction remain the most compelling arguments for the value of existing places and the desirability of cumulative accretion.

Jacobs prioritized the small scale of daily life as the generative component of good urbanism. However, the ideal on which she based her theories, New York City's Greenwich Village in the 1950s, now seems alarmingly singular in a world of superstores, malls, edge cities, doughnut downtowns, and suburban ghettos. These more recent forms of urban life, on close inspection, can also be seen to possess their own ethos and are ultimately as conducive to social life, ritual, and surprise as dense urban neighborhoods. They are

Jerde Partnership, Universal Studio's Citywalk, Los Angeles, 1992

also, with effort, equally susceptible to positive change. Despite her anthropological approach, Jacobs too quickly associated specific forms with good urbanism and defined those forms as good. With hindsight, this type of insular recursion too quickly devalues alternate urbanisms that inevitably are as dearly loved by residents as the routines and forms of Greenwich Village were admired by Jacobs. This parochialism can be explained in part by the goal of her pursuit: she was attempting to document the positive values of her street and neighborhood in order to keep them from being destroyed by a highway project. The absolutism of her observations nonetheless results in a non-inclusive theory of place-making that cannot encompass, observe, value, incorporate, or utilize a full urban spectrum.

During the time that *The Death and Life of Great American Cities* was being written, a few American professionals were developing new methodologies that valued the same types of urbanism honored by Jacobs. These individuals actualized what Jacobs had only theorized—a professional design activity based on urban context rather than on the clean slate that modernism took as its starting point. In the 1950s in Philadelphia, Edmund Bacon endeavored to rationalize the mingling of large-scale urban clearance schemes with the preservation and rehabilitation of exist-

ing neighborhoods. The plans he oversaw for Society Hill and Market Street exemplified the emerging movement to reconcile redevelopment with the formal relationships and social forces already at work in evolving cities. In New York City, Jonathan Barnett practiced an even more incremental approach to physical planning based on the extrapolation of existing city patterns. This understanding of urban morphology was used as the foundation for large-scale contextual master planning that was supported by strategic zoning incorporating financial encouragement for development. Barnett brought an architect's sensibility to incentive zoning and development deal-making, merging public policy, negotiation, and design into a powerful framework for the emergent professional practice of urban design. The expanded arena of activity that Barnett promulgated was separate from but related to architecture; different from yet analogous to landscape design; more three-dimensionally oriented than land-use planning; similar to, though less quantitatively rigorous than, real-estate development.

In essence, Bacon and Barnett promulgated a new role for the architect: urban policy-maker. In this role, the architect assumes little responsibility for actually building anything. Now operating as urban designers, these architects work only at the formative stages of projects, on almost equal standing with the political and business leaders who make projects happen. The urban designer contributes to the establishment of a quantifiable framework of economic, physical, and planning guidelines to which buildings are meant to conform through time. Notwithstanding devotion to the textures and flux of the daily life of the city as described by Jacobs, by emphasizing the pseudo-scientific in the building of cities, the urban designer's interest in the art of the city evolves inexorably into interest in the art of the deal. Not surprisingly, Bacon and Barnett made their strongest marks not as individual designers but as government officials or consultants orchestrating development deals and planning agreements.

The problem with this definition of the role of the urban designer is its reliance on design tools and actions that are never architecturally specific. The designer as policy maker too easily becomes a diagrammer of plans, disconnected from the daily palpability of the city. Physical architecture and the dynamics of place-making become less important than the social, environmental, transportation, economic, and legislative actions that surround building in the city. Though designers must proactively confront these intrinsic urban arenas, overemphasis on top-down programming and policy neglects to recognize or accommodate— and ultimately diminishes—the complex surprises that architecture can bring to the daily life of the city. At best this approach has occasionally enhanced daily life through acts of building preservation or through the adoption of vague guidelines for contextual architecture. At worst, this type of urban design, initially motivated by an appreciation of the existing city, has ironically become complicit in the production of homogeneous urban spaces, the ubiquitous "festival" marketplaces and "old towns" that dot the American urban landscape.

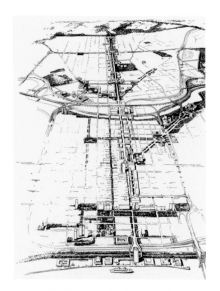

Edmund N. Bacon, redevelopment of Philadelphia, 1963

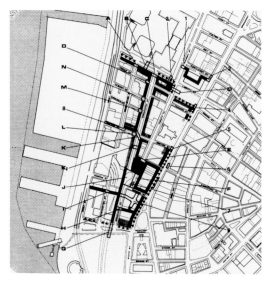

Jonathan Barnett, Greenwich Street Special Zoning District, New York, 1969

In contrast to Barnett's and Bacon's visions of professional urban design as strategic public policy are various attempts to replicate an organic urbanism through the architectural manipulation of building typologies. An influential advocate of this approach, Christopher Alexander, is known for his didactic rules that advocate piece-by-piece construction within small blocks. Moving beyond the professional facilitation espoused by Bacon and Barnett, Alexander described a design incrementalism explicitly related to democratic processes. In *A New Theory of Urban Design* (1987), Alexander blurred the distinction between urban designer and citizen, proposing that residents be an integral part of design in their community.

Rejecting the fixed and overarching master plan, Alexander suggested that each time a building was proposed, people should come together to analyze options and choose design directions collectively. Interacting through a chesslike process that is part neighborhood design workshop and part city-council meeting, participants in Alexander's process build an ever-evolving consensus for the role, scope, and scale of each new development as it occurs. Alexander's method demands that every building be crafted in response to existing physical and social patterns. At the same time, each building is expected to anticipate how the next stage of growth can be accommodated.

However, not completely trusting the realities of democratic organic city development, Alexander's pattern language also prescribes an exacting and unyielding set of design parameters based on traditional architectural typologies. What appear to be syntactic and pragmatic parameters of city building are actually a predefined semantics of urban form. Alexander's design typologies are in fact so specific that they invariably generate Italianate townscapes, as amply illustrated throughout *A New Theory of Urban Design*. If public discussions uncover desires for urban patterns or building types that fall outside Alexander's canon of self-posited timelessness (for instance, a shopping mall), these collective choices have no place within Alexander's standards of urban design. Alexander's approach is free of the predilection for overbearing master planning that has been associated with bureaucratic modernism, but it nevertheless turns out to be yet another pedagogy that reasserts the architect's personal taste and control.

Like Alexander, Kevin Lynch also sought to forge a normative language for urban design. In *The Image of the City* (1960), he developed an approach for mapping the psychogeographic forces of

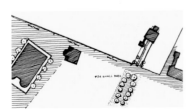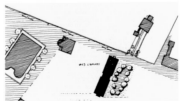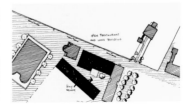

Christopher Alexander, small urban space formed building by building

the city. This process entails asking questions and making observations about the physical values of existing places, an investigation similar to those that inspired Team X.[5] Lynch's methodology visualizes with overlay maps and user surveys the same shaping forces that Alexander described, but without resorting to any formal design ideology. In *Good City Form* (1981), Lynch would further moderate the idea that there might be any one correct urban morphology and accept the propriety of markedly varying city forms as found in different regions, countries, and cultures. With this more inclusive point of view, Lynch identified seven traits of urban design: vitality, fit, sense, access, control, efficiency, and justice. As opposed to recommending actual forms that might conform to these traits, Lynch proclaimed a semantics of performance standards for urban design that could guide the public conversations that shape each city's form and thus provide a framework for the supposedly intelligent and democratic discussion of a range of choices. Utilizing Lynch, options specific to the arena under examination can be reiterated and rearranged, hopefully without prejudice, by the designer. Unlike Alexander, in Lynch's quest for an urban design language he addressed the semantic dimension of the city (and architecture) only after the syntactic and pragmatic dimensions were considered.

Though Lynch's method is less didactic than Alexander's because it avoids prescribing architecture, in practical applications the credibility of environmental design (and designers) becomes suspect without a commitment to form specifics, regardless of the quality of the syntactic framework or the inclusiveness of the debate. Lynch's performance standards are highly compelling as a way of building verbal consensus, but too little premium is placed on actual physical design. Though Lynch's process leads to agreements, in the absence of a specific design framework to support the words, urban design becomes a diminished force in the practical development of cities; in essence, a picture is still worth a thousand words.

Both Alexander and Lynch failed to

5
Smithson, TEAM 10 MEETINGS, 60-65, 68-69. Smithson says of Christopher Alexander, "Team X are all builders by nature and tend to be nervous—if not suspicious—of those who proceed from one research to another."

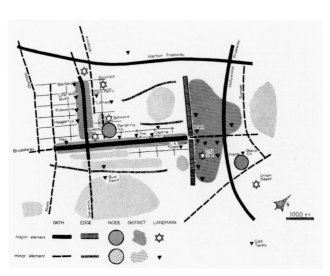

Kevin Lynch, psychogeographic mapping of downtown Los Angeles, late 1950s

6
Denise Scott Brown, URBAN CONCEPTS (New York: Academy Editions, 1990), 8-20.

synthesize successfully the complexity of the design act with the accretive acts of daily life, making it difficult to actually apply their theories. In her 1990 autobiographical essay "Between Three Stools: A Personal View of Urban Design Pedagogy," Denise Scott Brown specifically addressed the frustration associated with reconciling the planning of the social city with the design of a symbolic architecture.[6] She concluded that urban design, defined as a social architecture of "forms, forces, and functions," was a failure. Scott Brown further pointed to a deleterious stasis in the field: "Urban designers have been particularly slow to catch up with changes in theory in both architecture and planning. They are generally behind the times, when they should be the most up front. Little good theory and little intellectual and design leadership has come from the urban design community, academic or professional."[7] Operating from this perceived gap, Scott Brown has been able to synthesize an approach that employs the everyday forces of the city, whether physical or social, more

7
Scott Brown, URBAN CONCEPTS, 20.

than any other urban designer or architect trained in the period after World War II and before 1960. Unlike Team X, her bias in favor of the pedestrian-oriented street is more firsthand than conceptual. In contrast to Alexander, Scott Brown employs in her work a diversity of popular and elite architectural languages. Unlike Lynch, her commitment to exploring the nuances of architectural form is evident in the eye-level perspectives, sections, and elevations employed to endow the ideas with tangibility. Her proposals are necessarily more grounded in the everyday than are the view-from-above master plans associated with urban design as public policy. Nonetheless, Scott Brown still deplores the state of urban design and its theoretical underpinnings as more often than not denying the complex realities and pluralism of the city—this despite the fact that over the last forty years architects and urban designers have ceaselessly attempted to immerse themselves in the ethos of the everyday. For Scott Brown the fundamental question remains: is there an explicit way to incorpo-

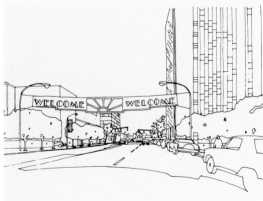

Venturi, Rauch & Scott Brown, Washington Avenue improvement proposals, Miami Beach, 1979

rate the social and experiential multiplicity of urban life into a practice of city design and architecture?

The generation of architects trained during the 1960s and 1970s has attempted to address this quandary with an even more architecturally explicit practice. These designers champion the production of individual buildings and places, over any type of planning process, as an urgent obligation of decision makers. Two poles define this design- and construction-oriented perspective: New Urbanism, and the work and writings of the architect Rem Koolhaas.

New Urbanism has derived from architects' and communities' renewed interest in history and regional difference as well as from a consciousness of issues of ecological sustainability. The most persuasive New Urbanists promote villagescapes of carefully disposed individual buildings exemplifying small-town values. Their urban design typically combines elements of the early-twentieth-century garden city and the nineteenth-century Main Street overlaid with fixed-rail transit. Paradoxically, even as local and regional typological precedent is sought for each project, this movement also subscribes to the myth of a nationally coherent urbanism. This gainsaying appeals to the consumers who buy homes in these communities, consumers who seek the stability of unifying forms and symbols in the face of increasingly pluralized metropolitan areas.

New Urbanists are indelibly associated with a single model that emphasizes low-density housing clustered around small civic spaces and town centers. This form replicates the multinucleated automobile suburbs built on open land during the 1920s without absorbing the consequences and lessons of the subsequent seventy years.[8] New Urbanism's ordered yet expansive pattern language, which demands large, blank slates of land, is ultimately antithetical to the chaotic parcel-by-parcel evolution, intensifying edge cities, and recycling suburbs of existing urban landscapes. Even as the ideal New Urbanist town promotes traditional values, the master-plan

8
For a review of New Urbanism writings see John Kaliski, "Reading New Urbanism," DESIGN BOOK REVIEW 37-38 (winter 1996-97): 69-80.

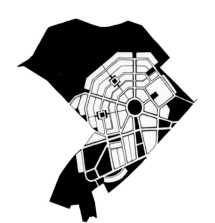

Andres Duany and Elizabeth Plater-Zyberk, pedestrian and open-space network of a village in Maryland, 1988

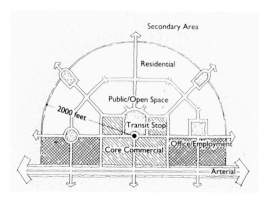

Peter Calthorpe, diagram of transit-oriented development

9
Rem Koolhaas
and Bruce Mau,
S,M,L,XL,
(New York: The
Monacelli Press,
1995), 1248.

10
Koolhaas and Mau,
S,M,L,XL, 1256.

11
Koolhaas and Mau,
S,M,L,XL, 1263.

12
For discussion of
the flaneur see
Walter Benjamin,
CHARLES BEAUDE-
LAIRE: A LYRIC POET
IN THE ERA OF HIGH
CAPITALISM (London:
Verso, 1983),
34-66. With
regard to the
flaneur Benjamin
writes, "The street
becomes a
dwelling for the
flaneur; he is as
much at home
among the facades
of houses as a citi-
zen is in his four
walls. To him the
shiny, enameled
signs of business
are at least as
good a wall orna-
ment as an oil
painting is to a
bourgeois in his
salon. The walls
are the desk
against which he
presses his note-
books; news-stands
are his libraries
and the terraces of
cafés are the bal-
conies from which
he looks down
on his household
after his work is
done."

mentality ironically turns its back on what already exists, needlessly limiting its potential for evolution. The so-called neotraditional town tugs at emotions and speaks to a mythologized memory of socially homogeneous innocence, of golden ages conveniently distant. Though New Urbanists have recently acknowledged the realities of denatured downtowns, inner cities, and older suburbs as a subject for inquiry and action, their approach is still dismissive of the present urban landscape. The nostalgia of New Urbanism, with its simulative building-by-building urbanism, results in a carelessness toward existing conditions that is ultimately as problematic as any other modern vision of urban renewal.

In his 1994 essay "The Generic City," Rem Koolhaas declares aspirations to create identity and character, the New Urbanist's mainstay, to be a "mousetrap . . . in which more and more mice have to share the original bait, and which, on closer inspection, may have been empty for centuries."[9] Though he shares with the New Urbanists a commitment to building as urban catalyst, Koolhaas is opposed to any form of architectural traditionalism, stressing the continued relevance of the giant forms and patterns of the global city. Airports, hotels, shopping centers, and theme parks, with their accompanying culture of capital accumulation and hyperactivity, fascinate and inspire him. He is also engrossed by these

urban forms' resistance to facile or fixed meaning: "The endless contradictions of these interpretations prove the richness of the Generic City."[10] Yet even as he embraces the Generic City, Koolhaas regrets that its forms have destroyed any semblance of civic memory, that "the Generic City perpetuates its own amnesia."[11]

For Koolhaas, the functionalism of the late-capitalist city is best addressed with an inexorably inefficient architecture and urbanism. At heart a nineteenth-century flaneur who gets more pleasure from the life of the sidewalks than from domestic regimen, Koolhaas willfully arranges the programs of his own designs to incorporate the social component of the urban street.[12] For instance, in the Kunsthal, in Rotterdam, completed in 1992, Koolhaas and O.M.A. projected a ramp-street directly through the middle of the building, connecting the park below to the street above. At its halfway point, the ramp opens directly into an auditorium that doubles as a foyer for the institution; the intellectual discussions contained within the walls of the auditorium thus spill directly onto the ramp as street, breaking down the physical barriers separating high culture from sidewalk culture. An architecture of social mixing complements an urbanism of daily place, realized within a structure that is simultaneously visually contemporary and generically "off-the-shelf" in its use of materials and detailing. Even though he creates a transparent architecture that reveals the social, Koolhaas nevertheless feels a void when contemplating a city of generic architecture: "Silence is now reinforced by emptiness: the image shows empty stalls, some debris that was trampled underfoot. Relief . . . it's over. That is the story of the city.˙ The city is no longer. We can leave the theater now."[13] Observation suggests, however, that the city as social theater framed by symbolic architecture is definitely not abandoned. Rather, the city of daily life is simply difficult to incorporate into built work given the means and concepts that architects typically use.

Whether willfully rejecting the past or blindly denying the present, Koolhaas and the New Urbanists respectively develop an urban design of architectural fixity that ultimately homogenizes the collective everyday. In both visions, the architecture of the city is consumed rather than inhabited: the New Urbanists retreat to mythohistoric narratives while Koolhaas's Generic City projects a hypermodern dystopia of city as shopping mall. The New Urbanists and

Koolhaas nevertheless demonstrate an ever-growing commitment to architecture in urban-design practice at precisely the moment when the reality, as opposed to the representation, of plural urbanism has emerged as a powerful force in the building of the contemporary city.

Throughout these varied debates and approaches, the importance and role of architecture, versus planning or urban design, in the processes of twentieth-century city creation and alteration have oscillated radically. In the city of a thousand voices, however, unilateral design theories of any sort are doomed to failure. The creation of this city is the grail that architects-as-urbanists have sought. As urban environments continue to evolve, designers must find new means of incorporating the elements that remain elusive: ephemerality, cacophony, multiplicity, and simultaneity. Architects and urban designers consistently flirt with these concepts only to reject them in favor of closed models of cities past, future, and utopian. Urban design must construct a practice and theory of architecture that can embrace the

13
Koolhaas and
Mau, S,M,L,XL,
1264.

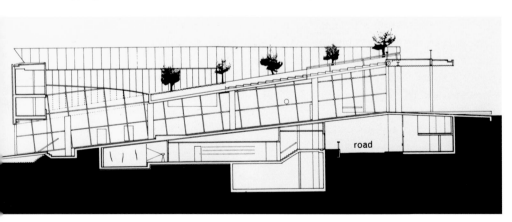

road

Rem Koolhaas/O.M.A., Kunsthal, Rotterdam, Netherlands, 1992

complexity that is the present city. In the absence of a commitment to this city, urban design and architecture may finally lose all relevance in the planning and making of urban places.

URBAN DESIGN AS PROFESSIONAL PRACTICE

The present city exists as a multilayered space shaped by the ebb and flow of personal and social politics, economics, and environmental conditions. At its best, urban design creates a physical framework for the present city's myriad activities. At its most questionable, urban design produces a narrow, dormant analogue of urban vitality, as abstract as transportation diagrams of a highway network or illustrations of capital flow between regions and continents. Despite its failures over the course of the twentieth century, urban design has nonetheless become the chief means through which architects have attempted to preserve the status of design as a social art.

As articulated by its practitioners, urban design requires a wide range of skills, including the ability to design environments that integrate nature into the city, to shape and enact ordinance-based design policies, to facilitate public debates, to serve as advocate for the disadvantaged and disgruntled, and to develop pattern languages of appropriate building typologies. All of these pursuits entail negotiation between the social, economic, political, and aesthetic

forces of the city, but in most cases the results have been marked by design essentialisms that deny the multiple human voices that comprise the everyday city. In spite of its reformist agenda and willingness to expose architecture to the vicissitudes of political processes, urban design is too frequently reduced to the creation of single-purpose monuments to power. When urban design is demoted to this role, the actual physical design of integrated places that reflect everyday desires becomes an afterthought to a misguided primacy of policy.

Architects and landscape architects do not typically feel equipped to relate physical design to the social, political, economic, and environmental flux that shapes the city. Especially in the United States, urban design is increasingly separated from these practices and is defined as a specialty in and of itself. Urban designers define themselves as leaders of teams that establish parameters and guidelines rather than as producers of specific designs. Despite a background in both design and planning, the urban designer is ironically neither planner nor architect. Decision makers and policy makers become confused, equating the conceptualization of the city and its attendant administration with the craft of city making.

Urban design fails and the role of the architect in the city is further diminished when the act of physical design disappears as a subject of public inquiry and creativity.

Without a commitment to making architecture and landscape in the context of the palpability and surprise of the present city, any type of urban design devolves into an intellectual curiosity distanced from its subject. At the same time, in the absence of any means of incorporating everyday urban life into the city, architecture and landscape architecture become marginalized, void of much purpose beyond the functional or purely aesthetic. Given this situation, a practice of city design that reconciles the intellectual abstraction of urban design and the formalism of architecture with the plural forces of the everyday city is insistently demanded.

FLIRTING WITH THE EVERYDAY

Rather than defining the unique physicalities of the particular, the "urban" describes a generalized condition or concept.[14] As typically practiced, urban design conceptualizes people in the city and then presumes to order their daily patterns from without. Immersed in this grand-scheme strategy as it has been over the last forty years, urban design has relied on metaphor, analogy, and planning processes rather than on the specifics of reality. This forces its practitioners to use instruments of abstraction, which are usually viewed as more powerful than physical actions when translated into policy.

Unlike urban design with its bird's-eye overview, architecture is conducted within a world of specific things. Even in a digital world, people do not escape from the need for shelter. Everyday lives take place in physical spaces that are marked by and through the presence of things. At its most basic, the city is a collection of things in space through which people wander during the course of their daily routines. Concentrated and spread out, centrifugal and centripetal, quiet and filled with noise, ordered and chaotic, the city is a contradictory but enveloping world of architectural objects placed in socialized space.

At the moment when the construction of everyday architectural things is necessary to the city design process, the urban designer who utilizes systems and the architect who seeks to order conceptually become practitioners of the general and fall back on policy, guidelines, and facilitation. The city's inhabitants, however, continue to use the elements, things, and spaces of the actual city. Over time, through individual and collaborative actions, each city's collection of everyday objects is reorganized, producing a specific and architectural spatial order that defies urban design. Whether master planned or not, the strategic city is continuously reinvented and physically marked by everyday activities, which are manifested in the built environment through architecture and landscape.

In the resulting city of tactics, design and architecture are everywhere, and each

14
Henri Lefebvre, WRITINGS ON CITIES, eds. Eleonore Kofman and Elizabeth Lebas (Cambridge, Mass.: Blackwell, 1996), 103.

15
Michel de Certeau,
THE PRACTICE OF
EVERYDAY LIFE
(Berkeley and Los
Angeles: University
of California
Press, 1988),
xvii–xx.

16
Spiro Kostof, THE
CITY ASSEMBLED: THE
ELEMENTS OF URBAN
FORM THROUGH
HISTORY (London:
Thames and
Hudson, 1992),
266.

17
Robert Caro, THE
POWER BROKER:
ROBERT MOSES AND
THE FALL OF NEW
YORK (New York:
Vintage Books,
1975), 849.

individual and group is a designer of the city.[15] The accretion of these architectural acts establishes an ephemeral building order for the city. The sometimes rapid yet often glacial changes and shifts in street plans combine with the ongoing activity of adding and deleting buildings to form frameworks for individual and collective creativity. The person who chooses a different commuting route, posts a sign over an existing sign, sells from a corner cart, or volunteers to organize a community meeting is as much a city designer as the developer and architect who construct a skyscraper or the city official who suggests an ordinance. The city is as much a consequence of these fluid everyday actions as of the overarching visions of urban designers who conceptualize fixed-in-time master plans.

The present city must be defined as a place of continuous creation. Its stories evade the manifold rationality of strategic urbanism, establishing traditions and histories that are both visible and waiting to be discovered. Reviled and desired, urban spontaneity challenges the logics of urban renewal, urban planning, urban redevelopment, urban design, and all of the other twentieth-century urbanisms that ignore existing things and places because of their imperfections. These stories and spontaneities, however flawed, constitute the everyday urban world.

The history of urban design suggests that for many the existing everyday world is more potent and beautiful than the ideal cities of professional urbanists, and worth fighting for. Referring to Paris, the historian Spiro Kostof notes that the evisceration of the medieval city, starting in the 1850s, for the building of boulevards generated much opposition.[16] A hundred years later, in reference to his crushing of concerted opposition to New York City highway construction, Robert Moses, without any concern for existing circumstances, said, "When you operate in an overbuilt metropolis, you have to hack your way with a meat ax."[17] In 1966 a small band of public-housing residents at Allen Parkway Village, in Houston, were defeated by the federal government after fifteen years of struggling to save their dilapidated but nevertheless National Register of Historic Places–listed homes. The destruction of this housing occurred despite the fact that hundreds of acres of privately held property lay fallow within walking distance. In each of these cases, and in thousands like them, big and small, local residents themselves generally do not view the potential of the existing city as an impediment to improvement. Indeed, there are powerful examples of modern art, literature, and cinema that have celebrated the sublime quality of these places in part because of the implicit creative, social, and intellectual freedom associated with the order of disorder. In contrast, urban design has never found a way to fully incorporate this dynamism into its practice, but instead has consciously or inadvertently promoted the annihilation of the existing city in the search for unitary truths.

The present city is a physical record of everyday acts and counteracts of decision making. The resulting physical record reveals the potential for a city design, as opposed to an urban design, that eludes classical aspirations of symmetry, order, and control. When urban design becomes city design it is transformed into an architecture of situational tactics in social space. Architecture as city design can become a discourse of collaboration. Alternative definitions of the city beautiful become possible as a multitude of voices are not only heard but sought out and maintained, in the physical artifact that is the architecture of the present city. If city design as situational architecture becomes a discourse of spatial tactics, city residents as well as architects and other specialists continually encounter one another in conversation to shape further what already exists.

City design as situational architecture acknowledges that each person and entity is constructing space and place with the acts of daily life. The architect as city designer is privileged to enter into these dialogues, helping to shape the frameworks within which these acts occur. Working to design the city in this manner, the acts of

the architect or planner cannot exist without the input of the city dweller. These interwoven tactical shifts play out in a continuous choreography of dialogue and creation. In a practice of city design, assumptions and priorities regarding the design of the city change, history reveals the present as much as the past, and the values of urban designers are challenged. City design's framework of continuous iteration demands that the architect as designer contribute skills first, and then knowledge, to a public that makes the city.

The methods, means, and aesthetics of this craft are barely defined, which makes the transition from theory to practice a difficult one. The architect in the present city must produce work that embraces spontaneous and discursive multiplicity. Yet what does this architecture feel and look like? Is it actually possible to deduce architecture—as opposed to incremental vernacular building—from immersion in the present city? Is the experience of the present—the daily ritual and dialogue of the everyday—sufficient inspiration for the materialization of the complexly beautiful?

REALITY

Architects and urban designers are typically taught to design toward stasis. Any notion of urban stability, however, is sooner or later contradicted by the city's inherent flux. Even when a designer eschews utopian visions, solitary acts of creation and planning, especially from the perspective of expert overview and authority, too easily devolve into the production of fixed ideals, which cannot address—much less acknowledge—the full panoply of daily city rhythms, acts, and debates.

Daily use of city places provokes responses and counter-responses to utopian visions. The result, the everyday cacophony of the city, is not traditionally defined as beautiful. When the designer begins with everyday reality and defines it as beautiful, existing situations become a starting point rather than a stumbling block. Reality, as opposed to utopian stability, provides inspiration.

From this inception, a practice of city design explicitly incorporates the voices, activities, signs, and symbols of daily life. The sum of daily transactions is recognized as an evolving material story to which both the city dweller and the designer must contribute. The realities of everyday life must saturate the entire planning and design process.

REASSEMBLY

City design seeks new meanings and invention through the recombination and extrapolation of present elements. Utilizing what already exists, city design is a form of bricolage. The city designer reassembles narratives of place in order to intensify and render more visible the ordinary stories of city life. Debate negotiates the process of combining individual and group narratives with the designer's arrangement of these narratives in objects and places. The city thus designed is the simultaneous city of everyday life, celebrated in modern literature and art and sought after but denied by modern architecture and urban design.

DIALOGUE

City design opens itself to the realities of each participating party. City design struggles to reveal commonalities as well as differences. The city is thus opportunistically grounded in its own memory even as it evolves. In the dialogue that reveals these differences, commonalities, and memories, the designer has a valuable and needed skill rather than an expert position or ideology. During debates, the designer participates by illustrating alternatives that incorporate the many voices, dreams, and desires of existing situations. The hyperinclusiveness of the resulting designs is dynamic. Proposals and counterproposals lead to completed projects that reflect and juxtapose commonalities and differences. City design proceeds tactically from the ground up to realize desired objects and places out of the debates and panoply of resulting choices.

THE IMPLOSION OF TIME

The reliance on functional or ideological prescriptions has for the most part eliminated from the contemporary planned city the very simultaneity sought by urbanists. Banal suburbs, shiny but empty downtowns, formal office parks, and abandoned districts result from policies that neither recognize the everyday nor allow it to assert and reassert itself. City design ferrets out, values, encourages, and intensifies the irregularities and juxtapositions of daily life with regard to both program and form. This counters the tendency of generic systems to overwhelm the life of the city with single-purpose constructions.

In the traditional city, simultaneity has only been achieved after generations of incremental change. The contemporary city, while often lacking this quality, seeks increasingly to preserve existing simultaneous situations or to simulate them when they are not available. City design generates, rather than simulates, simultaneity by incorporating the palpable city with its mundane routines and extraordinary events into the evolution of existing places. City design accepts the new, the old, the present, the simulated, and the spectacular within a framework of everyday situations. Through the insistent inclusion of these factors in the making of the city, city design implodes time to achieve urban vitality.

FROM URBAN DESIGN TO ARCHITECTURAL DESIGN

The movement from urban design toward city design entails a nuanced but critical shift in emphasis on the part of the urban designer. Critical to this evolution is the recognition of architecture's important role in establishing the human context of everyday life as well as a recommitment to the validity of city making through specific acts of architecture. The amenability and quality of housing, open spaces, and places of work, play, and education are natural components of city design rather than aesthetic fore- or after-thoughts on the part of policy makers and urban designers.

The architecture of city design engages the daily without abandoning interest in structure, form, typology, light, material, and the histories of the art. These elements instead provide a vocabulary for public conversations about quality of life.

The architecture that accompanies a practice of city design must also communicate with the inhabitants of a place. To construct a communicating city means to provide spaces within buildings and landscapes where both programmatic and symbolic points of difference and commonality are expressed. These places include overlays of new and old architecture that express plural histories and memories as well as understanding the topology and tectonics of a locale.

THE PRESENT CITY AND
THE PRACTICE OF CITY DESIGN

City design recognizes that every act has the capacity to adjust in order to tell a better and more ethical story. In its actual and nonidealized vitalities, situations, and forms, the present city demands to be the starting point for this story. Urban planning and design efforts over the last century have rarely—and only unintentionally—stumbled upon an inclusive everyday practice of city design. The present city insists upon such a practice. By defining the city beautiful as the situational bricolage of daily life and debate, all individuals have the capacity to contribute to the design and improvement of their city. In turn, those who elect to become professional city designers must also commit themselves to the practice of architecture. Urban design as phenomenon, practice, and profession must be subsumed by architecture, and in turn architects must be moved, shaped, and inspired by the everyday present city.

The present city demands to be the starting point

JOHN CHASE

THE GIANT REVOLVING (WINKING) CHICKEN HEAD

AND

THE DOGGIE DRINKING FOUNTAIN:

MAKING SMALL DISTINCTIVE PUBLIC

SPACES

ON PRIVATE LAND

BY USING

COMMONPLACE OBJECTS

As the home of the Sunset Strip and a regional mecca for gays and lesbians, West Hollywood is hardly an average small town. But even in this two-square-mile area sandwiched between Beverly Hills and Hollywood, with a population of only thirty-six thousand, responding to and accommodating everyday life is an important objective for urban design. Because of West Hollywood's location and heavy traffic—both automotive and pedestrian—new development projects often include modest amenities that enhance the everyday life of the pedestrian as well as theatrical, expressive, or dramatic ornaments that register from passing automobiles.

In stark contrast to other areas in Southern California, one of the city's chief urban-design goals is to make it easier and more pleasant for people to be on the streets. West Hollywood's urban-design policies attempt to encourage the relationships that flourish between pedestrians on the street, relationships that are virtually impossible between motorists. In an urban environment dominated by commercial strips developed along heavily trafficked major boulevards, it is neither possible nor desirable to make the cars disappear; they are an essential part of any vital Southern California cityscape. It is feasible, however, to promote sidewalk activity that is strong enough to compete with automotive activity. The aspects of everyday life that can be incorporated into the public sidewalk—from bus-bench advertising to parking-lot landscaping—ideally function as development details that make the street habitable. These small-scale features complement the more spectacular urban-design elements that are oriented toward the automobile.

Pedestrian amenities make sense only if someone is on the sidewalk to use them. Again in contrast to other areas in Southern California, in West Hollywood at least three distinct groups experience their community on foot. These inveterate walkers include the city's Russian immigrants (approximately 13 percent of the population); gay and lesbian residents (approximately 30 percent of the population); and patrons visiting Sunset Strip rock clubs, gay establishments on Santa Monica Boulevard, and West Hollywood's other hotels, restaurants, and bars.

Improving everyday pedestrian life entails installing a diversity of features and activities that people can use on a regular basis. Motorists whiz past the sidewalks—they cannot interact tangibly with the streetscape as they speed by. Pedestrians can participate in their environment on a moment-by-moment basis—ancillary activities can be easily incorporated into a journey on foot. Well-equipped public pavements can be as hospitable to human beings as good interior public spaces. Common street objects such as bus shelters, drinking fountains, mailboxes, pay phones, newspaper vending machines, and dog-walking amenities give pedestrians a richer program of possible activities for a sidewalk sojourn and strengthen the bond between strollers and the streetscape.

West Hollywood is a valuable location for businesses because of its lively mix of residential and commercial use. The area's adjacency to Beverly Hills and a high concentration of design showrooms, hotels, nightclubs, bars, and restaurants make it a vital urban center. Because of this desirability, the city is able to ask for public improvements in exchange for granting developers the right to locate their projects in West Hollywood. The city's urban-design policies are focused on strengthening the relationships between development projects and their surroundings. Buildings in West Hollywood must have front entrances that face the street rather than rear entrances that lead to the parking lot. Facades must have enough windows so that passersby can get a sense of interior activity.

At the city's behest, developers have recently begun to provide tiny plazas adjacent to the public sidewalk as a benefit to walkers. These miniature parks, accessible to all, effectively extend the public space of the sidewalk. They are often carved out of the mandatory landscaped buffer around parking lots, a perimeter that is legally required to be at least five feet wide. In some cases, these plazas also respond to

the automobile with the inclusion of bold, large-scale elements that read clearly at twenty or thirty miles per hour. These elements often reflect the glamour, excitement, and creativity that residents and tourists alike expect from businesses in a community distinguished by the strong presence of both the entertainment and design trades. Incorporating the spectacular into signage or architectural elements vitalizes a project's relationship with motorists. And because car accommodations are always required for new developments, parking lots and their required buffering strips of landscaping offer an ideal opportunity to insert on private land public areas for pedestrians.

KOO KOO ROO

There are no better bodies than those to be found in West Hollywood. The demands of the marketplace, both romantic and industrial, keep West Hollywood's gay men, single women, actors, and actresses buff and trim. Low-fat diets and high-intensity exercise are the standard doctrine. Many West Hollywoodites exercise at one of two large gyms, both on Santa Monica Boulevard east of La Cienega. Just across the street, at the corner of West Knoll and Santa Monica, gym-goers dine post-workout at Koo Koo Roo, a chain restaurant for the health-conscious that specializes in skinless chicken and plenty of vegetables both raw and cooked.

There was room in the restaurant's required parking-lot landscaping to develop a small, partially paved area next to the sidewalk, the logical place to situate the phone booths, a drinking fountain, a bicycle rack, and seating, all set beneath a row of shade trees. Because most of the neighborhood exercisers walk to their workouts several times a week, this has become a see-and-be-seen section of the boulevard.

When Koo Koo Roo decided to locate in West Hollywood, one of the chief problems was how to reconcile the chain's need for a consistent corporate identity—as represented by the Koo Koo Roo chicken emblem—with the city's policy of discouraging new buildings on Santa Monica Boulevard that are cookie-cutter franchise clones. Fast-food restaurants that are aesthetic clones of their sibling restaurants across the country weaken the eclectic, distinctive urban character of the town.

Koo Koo Roo first proposed the installation of an enclosed corner tower bearing its standard two-dimensional chicken-head logo. To Koo Koo Roo, this logo represents a dependable standard of quality. The city asked the company to create a more original version of the logo, one that reflected the inventive design atmosphere of West Hollywood. Koo Koo Roo responded with a three-dimensional, revolving, and winking chicken head that looks like a giant toy. A generic piece of corporate signage

thus became memorable and unique to the area. The readily recognizable image of the winking chicken takes on greater power as a symbol, strong enough to take its place alongside other unforgettable media symbols such as the Michelin Man or the RCA Victor dog. Because it is exclusive to West Hollywood, the winking chicken assumes the informal landmark status that frequently characterizes Southern California promotional installations, as exemplified by such famous beacons as the Sunset Strip's giant Marlboro man and the now demolished whirling Sahara showgirl. The three-dimensional logo speaks to the passing motorist, while Koo Koo Roo's plaza becomes part of the activity pattern and life of the passing pedestrian.

GELSON'S MARKET

Gelson's Market is a neighborhood supermarket at the corner of Kings Road and Santa Monica Boulevard. The area it serves, a densely developed residential section of West Hollywood, has more condominiums and elderly residents than any other neighborhood in West Hollywood and is unusually genteel. Residents walk their visibly well-loved dogs beneath the shady canopy of the mature oak and camphor trees on Kings Road.

In the corner of the Gelson's parking lot, next to the sidewalk, a tiny public area has been created for these citizens to enjoy. The small plaza is nestled into a gap

created by the layout of the angled parking spaces. Rather than absorbing the extra area into merely ornamental parking-lot landscaping, however, the designers chose to complement and extend the public space of the sidewalk. Two seats flank a drinking fountain with individual spigots for adults, children, and dogs. The little plaza is a destination point for local walkers, marking the heavily trafficked crossroads of quiet, dignified Kings Road and busy Santa Monica Boulevard. An overhead trellis defines the space and relates it to the trellis that shields Gelson's main entry. Landscaping rounds out the sense of enclosure and welcome. The plaza is just large enough to be habitable, the equivalent of setting a sofa on the front porch to take in the passing scene. Focused by an unusual feature, the canine drinking fountain, the space enlivens the quotidian activity of walking the dog and becomes a social gathering point.

SHERIFF PLAZA

I would like to suggest the possibility for one more of these small but eminently amenable public spaces, at the corner of Santa Monica and San Vicente Boulevards. This intersection is already one of the world's great gay intersections. When the AIDS Ride bicycle tour returns from San Francisco to West Hollywood, the crowd gathers at this corner. People assemble here in protest when yet another bill is

introduced to limit rights according to sexual orientation. This stretch of Santa Monica Boulevard is one of the few places in Los Angeles where the nighttime foot traffic is so dense that pedestrians actually have to slow down to avoid bumping into each other.

On the southeast corner of this intersection sits the West Hollywood station of the Los Angeles County Sheriff's Department, which has traditionally been more tolerant toward gays than the LAPD— the city police department. Because there are no windows in either of the station's two street facades, however, many passers-by had no idea the station was there. In order to call attention to the building and

its purpose, the city raised onto a pole a three-by-three-foot neon sign created in the form of a sheriff's badge. (The sign is a duplicate of one erected at Universal Studio's Citywalk, an urban entertainment center.) The icon stands on a small, triangular landscaped area left over by a corner indentation in the station's brick walls. The star-shaped sign is a spectacular object that changes the corner dramatically, communicating a sense of public security with its neon symbolism. It reminds pedestrians how close they are to the station's protection.

The sign points to a perfect and untapped opportunity for public space. If a little bit of the area around the sign were to be paved, the site could accommodate such amenities as a bulletin board for communication between the sheriff's department and local residents, a drinking fountain, seats, and telephone booths, all of which would facilitate casual use of the space. Strollers could reconnoiter and take stock here on the way to or from the area's stores, bars, and restaurants. By providing a spot to linger, the space would acknowledge the importance of being out in the public world. It is especially desirable to create this kind of corner pedestrian oasis here, since the two intersecting boulevards are so wide, and intervals between changes in the traffic signals so long, that crossing can be quite daunting.

BILLBOARD GARDENS

Billboard Gardens is a project currently under development that has the potential to incorporate both everyday and spectacular elements. The proposed complex will be built on a narrow lot that slopes from Sunset Boulevard to a residential street below. As presently constituted, Billboard Gardens would split the site into three zones. Apartment housing would take up the southernmost zone, along the residential street. Private gardens for the apartment dwellers would abut the building, with public gardens above; this landscape would be designed according to a strong theme or central concept, such as a Persian garden or a scented or hanging garden.

Above the gardens to the north would be a commercial plaza facing Sunset Boulevard, the entrance flanked by billboards incorporated into a triumphal arch; from the inside, the arch would frame a view of the city below. Extending from the outside sidewalk, the plaza would have such space-efficient amenities as a newsstand, a small restaurant, and coffee and ice-cream stands. People who did not patronize the stands could nonetheless visit the plaza's terrace, making it a truly public space. Citizens could come here to take in the view (the only public space on the entire strip where one might do so), play cards, checkers, or chess, read the newspaper, or perhaps watch an outdoor television set tuned to the city's cable channel. Billboard Gardens would simultaneously serve as housing, pedestrian amenity, and public spectacle for the motorist.

TOP TEN REASONS WHY LITTLE TINY SPACES ON GREAT BIG BOULEVARDS ARE A GOOD IDEA

1. They slow down the urban pace. Commercial strips are all about getting from one destination to another in a car. Liberating to the public various nooks and crannies gives pedestrians a spot to stop and linger.

2. They don't charge admission. Anybody is free to use these spaces, even without patronizing the sponsoring store or restaurant. They really are public spaces, even if they sit on private land.

3. They are infinitely flexible. These spaces are created as the opportunity arises, and they can be readily altered to fit changing circumstances. They are part of developments created to accommodate particular businesses, but they can be remodeled or replaced to suit new establishments or needs. In that sense, they provide ad hoc situational opportunities for businesses responding to consumers' desires for novelty and innovation.

4. They're cheap, at least in comparison to other kinds of development. There is no land cost, normally one of the greatest expenses in the provision of public amenities, because these areas are located on a portion of the site that must already be set aside for the legally required parking-lot landscaping. Features such as small, paved patios, benches, and special lighting are relatively minor capital improvements. Finally, because the areas themselves are quite small—sometimes as tiny as a standard parking space—their cost per square foot is not multiplied by a high number.

5. They benefit everyone, private interests included. The tiny public pedestrian spaces, civic improvements that clearly encourage people to explore and enjoy a neighborhood, enhance the overall perceived value of a street. The private sphere indirectly benefits from this enriched value but also reaps tangible reward from increased patronage.

6. They make neighborhood residents more amenable to commercial development. In densely populated areas of Los Angeles such as West Hollywood, where commercial and residential uses cohabitate, new development virtually always backs up against residentially zoned land. Whether or not it is within legal zoning rights, new development is often unwelcome to residents. They fear the attendant increase in noise, traffic, and scarcity of parking. Such protests can delay, amend, or prevent proposed developments. Creating these miniature spaces might not answer primary quality-of-life concerns, but they can provide some benefit to a densely developed urban area.

7. They humanize the street. Thoroughfares with heavy vehicular traffic often become a no-man's-land. Residents feel neither attached to nor responsible for this indifferent, disposable environment. Public amenities associated with private establishments and situated next to sidewalks make sections of the street seem more occupiable. These bits of pavement become an extension of the walkers' home territory.

8. They involve the private sector in the public good. There are few ways to induce private businesses and their architects to think about and provide for the general public. This is one of them, and it is relatively painless.

9. They accommodate equal-opportunity aesthetics. The pedestrian nook tinkers with land use rather than with architectural style.

Communities such as West Hollywood base their identities on the free and energetic expression of individual people, businesses, and organizations. That is why West Hollywood was never swallowed up by Los Angeles, and why for many years it was reluctant to incorporate as a city. Just as it is impossible to imagine literature without a variety of characters, so is it difficult to conceive of a city like West Hollywood without both architectural hetero- and homogeneity. Pedestrian amenities do not impose a particular style or aesthetic on a sponsoring project. And regardless of the affinity any one passerby feels for the architectural vocabulary of a project, that passerby can still benefit from its pedestrian relationships and amenities.

10. They encourage diverse social encounters and help attract tourism. West Hollywood is home to two completely different cultures that are well versed in pedestrian life. Both the gay and lesbian and the Russian immigrant communities are experienced at creating vibrant street life, even under difficult circumstances. The city has the potential to help develop a third category of pedestrians—tourists. The increasing prominence of clubs, restaurants, and hotels in West Hollywood has great potential to contribute to a lively pedestrian environment.

PHOEBE WALL WILSON

A DAY IN THE LIFE
OF A
NEIGHBORHOOD

PLACE

Aerial of existing Linda Vista scho
library, and residential neighborho

LINDA VISTA, PASADENA, CALIFORNIA

Steam hisses from the coffee cart's espresso machine into the cold morning air. A mother rushes her child into school then walks across the plaza to drop her book into the library's return slot. She buys a newspaper and orders a cappuccino from the teenager who works there for an hour each day as part of the high school's work-study program. She jokes with him about his haircut.

On the patio, she takes a seat and joins a small group of parents who are heatedly discussing last night's meeting of the neighborhood association. They don't talk long; she and two others soon leave to car-pool to work. The remaining two walk back to their home offices. Each of them will find an excuse to return to the Neighborhood Place during the day, one to buy milk and cat food from the mobile convenience van that parks next to the plaza each day at three o'clock, and the other to spend a half hour listening to a second-grader read out loud.

Later, a semi-retired executive, now working part-time as a consultant, walks into the library and for two hours conducts research on the Internet at one of several computer carrels. He helps a college student having trouble with the fax system to submit an assignment and then goes out-

side for some tea. The man laughs to himself as he remembers that the college student's mother taught typing to his son in high school. In those days, he couldn't even type himself, and considered it a waste of time for his son to learn. Times change. As he leaves to return home, city workers are already putting up lights for that evening's performance and placing orange cones that will alert drivers to stay off the street plaza. Soon a group of parents and caregivers arrive at the tot lot with their charges. They eat lunch and converse in sentence snatches while they take turns maintaining peace and safety among the children.

In the afternoon, three teenage boys hop off their skateboards, buy sodas from the espresso cart, and hang around to watch the performance preparations. With interest, they eye two girls leaving the library; the girls cross the court and sit with their backs to the boys, their feet up on the edge of the fountain. A wave of kids runs out from the grade school onto the playground to join the after-school programs. A smaller group of children comes with a teacher to the fountain, where several of their parents have been waiting, talking and drinking coffee.

This whole scene takes place in the half-block-long area between the elementary school and the library in the middle of a single-family neighborhood. The chain-link fences, once the predominant feature of the schoolyard, have been nearly eliminated or made invisible under greenery. Fountains, seating, and water-efficient planting, all of them projects of the community and the PTA, have replaced the buckling asphalt. The newly inviting spot, with its other amenities and facilities, has been transformed into a neighborhood hub.

LOS ROBLES, CLEVELAND, OHIO

A widow leaves her apartment above an old carriage house to open up the main house. A small group is already waiting on the porch, and she greets most of them by name. The house is a large, historic structure. Its kitchen, back porch, and servants quarters have been converted into a laundromat and the comforting smell of clean clothes wafts through the rooms.

The living room harbors a small café that opens onto the porch. The widow tidies up clutter from last night's meeting and is ready to take care of her customers. The man who owns the telecommuting center upstairs comes in. They complain about the smog, and he tells her that the school district has expressed interest in renting the center as a computer study hall where he would conduct classes.

In the "City Hall Annex," as the dining room is now called, are an automated-teller machine, a self-service post office, and two computer terminals that have access to the library system and to an on-line list of all the events and services of the city. The terminals silently beckon in three languages.

Outside, the mobile convenience van has been parked for an hour between the street plaza and the bus stop on the corner. Next door, a few retirees putter in their vegetable plots, exchanging tools and friendly banter; they await the schoolchildren who will come for their gardening class. After loading laundry, two mothers sit under a jasmine-covered pergola. They watch their young children play in the tot lot in front. They come here two, maybe three times a week, sure to find a friend and, if a need arises, lend a hand to or get help from a neighbor.

The community police officer stops by to talk with one of the women about her teenage son. There is less crime in the neighborhood now that this Neighborhood Place exists. People drive more slowly in order to cross the street plaza. Neighbors recognize and speak to each other more frequently. Tomorrow there will be a market on the plaza during the day and a family dance in the evening.

This scene takes place on two residential lots and on a section of specially raised street in front of them. The shade trees distinguish the plaza as a unique space in the midst of small single-family homes and low-density apartments and townhouses.

THE BIRTH OF A CONCEPT: ENVISIONING THE NEIGHBORHOOD PLACE

In the 1970s and 1980s, my friends and I sought the vibrancy of urban life, naturally wary of the soullessness of the suburbs where many of us had spent sanitized, 1950s-style childhoods. As a young architect in San Francisco, I walked to work and could drop into no fewer than five coffee houses on the same block as my North Beach office, sure to run into friends or at least nodding acquaintances. When I needed a critique I could call on any of a handful of colleagues to walk over and take a look at my work in exchange for lunch or a drink in the evening. But now that we've married and had children, my city friends and I find ourselves returning to the suburbs, seeking space, gardens, and at least the perception of safety for our families.

Still, we miss the opportunities for spontaneous contact with others, even more so if we happen to be among the growing number of people working at home. We need a focus and a heart for our neighborhoods, and sometimes we need a cup of espresso—not made and sipped in the loneliness of our own kitchens. We want a place where we can connect again, what Ray Oldenburg in *The Great Good Place* (1989) calls that "third place," neither work nor home but one of the hangouts and gathering spaces that "get you through the day."

Longing for the sense of community and connection of the city, I sought to develop a family-oriented version of this network as an antidote for the alienation of suburban neighborhoods. The idea is a simple fix—clustering civic services such as libraries or schools with community-oriented commercial amenities, whether coffee carts, laundromats, or computer facilities, along with open space, right in the middle of residential neighborhoods.

Such a cluster would be called a "Neighborhood Place," and would function as a method to install a heart in existing residential neighborhoods. Through community consensus, neighbors could choose fine-grained urban design and land-use modifications to strengthen existing neighborhood relationships and create places where people of all ages could gather and converse as well as meet some of their daily needs.

IMPLEMENTING NEIGHBORHOOD PLACES

In 1992 the city of Pasadena undertook a complete overhaul of the land use and mobility elements of its general plan. I was chairperson of the city's planning commission. After hearing some three thousand residents talk about how they wanted to live, work, and get around, I crafted a clause that would allow Neighborhood Places to be created in residential areas—a small but radical departure from normal suburban zoning.

Policy 1.7 states:

> Neighborhood Centers: In order to provide a focus and community center for neighborhoods, [the city will] encourage the clustering of community-oriented services and amenities in and near residential neighborhoods, including schools, branch libraries, open space and parks including tot lots, and limited neighborhood commercial uses.

Over the next two years, my associate, Paige Norris, and I developed the concept in order to better demonstrate how it might be implemented. From the start, we realized that the idea would never receive public support if it was seen as some sort of outside, developer-driven project. Families would not accept the imposition of obviously commercial enterprises in their residential neighborhoods.

Nor could the development of a Neighborhood Place be seen as another city-sponsored plan. Unfortunately, because of the lasting scars of early, disruptive "community redevelopment projects," city planners are considered by some to fall in the same category as developers. But give neighborhoods the say as to what, if, and how a commercial use will be incorporated around, say, a school or a library, and I believe the results will be quite different.

COMPARISON OF DEVELOPER-DRIVEN VERSUS
NEIGHBORHOOD-BASED DEVELOPMENT

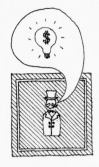 DEVELOPER

 NEIGHBORHOOD

Defines Development Scheme

Identifies Need

Buys/Leases Land

Locates Place

Directs Design

 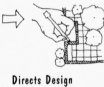

Directs Design

Seeks Approvals

Facilitates Approvals

Seeks Financing

Solicits Micro-Business

Sells/Operates Project

Enjoys Project

For this reason, we came up with a kind of ground-up, inverted development model that communities themselves could use in creating their own Neighborhood Places. Instead of a developer getting an idea for a project, finding the land, obtaining the land-use approvals (sometimes over the neighborhood's objections), securing financing, and, finally, opening to indifferent users, the whole process starts with the neighborhood itself. Rather than razing buildings or beginning with a preexisting blank slate, a civic structure of some sort (school, library, post office) provides an anchoring location and building block.

The neighborhood begins by determining if and what services or amenities it wants. With the cooperation of the city and local institutions, it works out the land-use agreements and conditions of operation and solicits the commercial components it wants. The invited businesses or the newly organized cooperative would then find itself in the unique position of having ready and willing patronage and civic permissions already in place. This is what "community development" ought to be but rarely is.

In order to show what a Neighborhood Place could be, Paige Norris and I knew that it was crucial to use photographs of real places, not just "artists' conceptions" or verbal planning jargon. People want to know what things will look and feel like before they become comfortable with change.

Suggest to people today that they might enjoy a "convenience store" in their neighborhood and they will most likely recoil in horror, envisioning a 7-Eleven-type store with garish Day-Glo advertising and gum-strewn, oil-soaked parking in front. Show them a photograph of a well-kept old house with a mom-and-pop market where the owners actually know the names of the customers and, if they are old enough, they might recall some establishment from their youth with a smile and say, "Sure, that would be great. We could use that here."

Physically and conceptually, we felt that there were three key ingredients of a Neighborhood Place: a civic presence of some sort; an open space, no matter how small; and a commercial enterprise. The civic presence of a library, elementary school, or post office would establish the Neighborhood Place firmly in the public domain. A mini-mall, for instance, could never become a Neighborhood Place because, fundamentally, the public is always a guest there.

Open space, like a civic institution, is important because of its public character and because it allows for the spontaneous gathering of groups of people. Most open spaces, such as school playgrounds, pocket parks, community gardens, and empty lots, are also the realm of children; kids can make noise, messes, and movements outdoors that would be frowned on inside

CIVIC PRESENCE

OPEN SPACE

NEIGHBORHOOD PLACE

MICRO-COMMERCIAL

Mary's Store convenience market, Sierra Madre

7-Eleven convenience market, Pasadena

Stratford Court fast food, Del Mar

McDonald's fast food, Pasadena

COMPONENT	USE	TYPICAL USER AGE						
		Infants & Todlers	Preschoolers	Grade Schoolers	Teenagers	Young Adults	Mid-life Adults	Seniors
Open Space	Park							★
	Plaza							
	Performance Stage / Arena							
	Community Garden							
	Tot Lot							
	Swimming Pool							
	Game Field / Court							
	Cemetery							
Civic	Library							★
	Community Center							
	Post Office							
	Pre-school / Childcare							
	Elementary School							
	Jr./ Sr. High School							
	College / University							
	Fire Station							
Commercial	Cafe							★
	Market / General Store							★
	Laundromat							
	Computing / Printing							
	Newsstand / Bookstore							
	Farmers' Market							
Mobility	Foot							★
	Stroller							
	Wheelchair							
	Bicycle							
	Roller blade / Skates							
	Skateboard							
	Motorcycle / Motorscooter							
	Automobile							
	Jitney							★
	Bus							★
	Rail							★

Diagram Showing Uses and User Ages

buildings. These places provide a link to the natural world, to the elements of earth, air, and growth denied by human-made structures.

The third ingredient, a commercial enterprise such as a fresh-juice stand, laundromat, or farmers market, has the potential to become a touchstone for our daily lives. There is also a kind of dignity in the repeatedly renewed contract of a daily exchange of money for goods and services: "I will come here regularly and pay you for things that I need because you provide what I want at prices that I think are fair." Simple free-market enterprise, writ small.

The ideal Neighborhood Place should be like a mini–town square. When you are there you get the sense that you are at the heart of things, that this is the place you would come to celebrate a public event or

to seek help and solace in the event of a disaster. The purpose in combining the three ingredients—whether a café and library next to a park, a police substation and telecommuting center near basketball courts, or a farmers market on part of an elementary school playground—is to provide a balance of vitality and stability. A good Neighborhood Place should make people's lives richer, safer, and more convenient and enjoyable, and should strengthen the bonds of community.

MAKING ONE PLACE A REALITY

After our daughter was born, I searched in vain for a place to walk to on weekends where I might meet other neighborhood parents. I began eyeing the ill-used bits of playground at the nearby fenced-in elementary school, transforming them in my mind

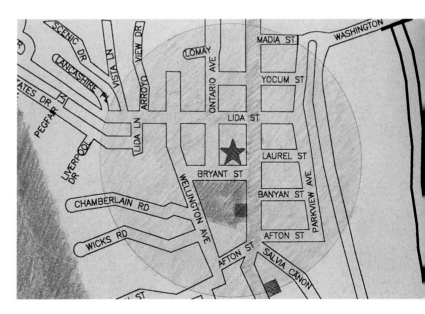

Seeds for Neighborhood Place: school, library, residential neighborhood; yellow circle shows quarter-mile radius

into tot lots or micro-parks. Not surprisingly, it was this school and adjacent branch library that we adopted as a case-study site when Paige Norris and I wanted a real locale to illustrate the Neighborhood Place.

As urban designers, we had taken the show on the road, stumping the concept at the national meeting of Neighborhoods USA and at other planning conventions. But no group or city had come forward wanting us to help develop a Neighborhood Place in their neighborhood. We were dying to do one.

Our initial design ideas for the Linda Vista Neighborhood Place included the creation of a street plaza between the library and the school: by raising the street to the level of the sidewalk, it could be closed off for community events but could also be driven on slowly at other times. We also proposed removing some of that ill-used asphalt to provide my longed-for tot lot and a landscaped area where parents could wait for their schoolchildren. We suggested that a somewhat derelict patio next to the library be transformed into a café and gathering spot. There was even a plot of land that could be cultivated into a community garden.

We presented these ideas and before-and-after photographs and drawings to a group of Linda Vista neighbors, not without some trepidation. We were putting forth a preconceived scheme that we—not the community—had concocted. Not only did this have great potential for rejection, but it stood in direct opposition to the model we'd been touting for development, wherein desire for the Neighborhood Place and its specific components had to come from the community. The proposals were met with lots of talk, excitement, doubts, and "It'll never happen in this neighborhood" comments.

Linda Vista Elementary School

The local neighborhood association formed a Neighborhood Place subcommittee, chaired by an enthusiastic new mother, Reneé Marino, who was temporarily on leave from her job in strategic planning. But nothing concrete came of it. I lost hope of anything happening in the area, turning my attention to other neighborhoods.

Then early in the summer of 1996 a flyer fell out of my morning newspaper announcing the opening of the Coffee Café on Saturday mornings at the Linda Vista branch of the Pasadena Public Library. The Neighborhood Place committee had worked with the neighborhood-association board and obtained a temporary permit from the city to open a café staffed by volunteers from the neighborhood. For the whole summer and well into the fall, every Saturday phone numbers were exchanged for pet sitting, heated discussions were had about the use of the nearby Rose Bowl stadium, and children had fun playing with each other on the playground or hanging around at the café with their parents, who enjoyed hanging around themselves.

The following summer, the café attracted a private operator to run the espresso cart and had the wholehearted support of the library in plans to remodel and relandscape the courtyard. The neighborhood association started talking about the possibility of adding onto the library and permanently incorporating the café in the addition. The school principal, the PTA, and the neighborhood association are discussing the possibility of opening up the grounds to the neighborhood after school and on weekends on a year-round basis. There is even talk of operating the café at the school on weekday mornings. This Neighborhood Place is taking on a life of its own. As it should.

Proposed Neighborhood Place

Linda Vista Library

School field

Library terrace café, street court, gathering place

School, community garden

School playground corner

Tot lot

NORMAN MILLAR

STREET SURVIVAL:

THE PLIGHT

OF
THE

LOS ANGELES

STREET VENDORS

This essay tells a story about architects working with a group of people to help them improve their everyday lives on the streets of Los Angeles. The story unfolds against a complex and open-ended socio-political drama that plays out bit by bit over a period of several years. In contrast to "politically correct" advocacy architecture of the 1960s, here the architect plays an ordinary and nonpivotal role. The approach supports light-handed and localized tactics to strengthen urban life and economic community through constantly shifting collaborations. The techniques empower voice over form and challenge conventional modes of architectural work. Finally, this tale demonstrates the difficulties and ambiguities of indeterminate work in a social setting where the architectural outcome is unknown and, if successful, likely to be invisible.

MACARTHUR PARK

MacArthur Park, a once genteel neighborhood in Los Angeles, is one of the most densely populated areas in the country. Located just west of downtown, the area is also known as Westlake. In the early 1900s, MacArthur Park's grand hotels made it a favorite desti-nation for vacationers from the Midwest and East Coast, and in the mid-1900s, Westlake emerged as a bohemian enclave, home to many artists and a center for labor unions. Today most of the area's residents are

Central Americans who immigrated to escape strife in their homelands or to seek Southern California's economic opportunities. In the mid-1980s, affordable crack cocaine arrived in MacArthur Park, bringing with it a sad trail of easy addiction and ruined lives. As the area became known for its accessible drug supply, the local homeless population grew, especially within the park itself and on surrounding streets. The southern portion of the park was subsequently closed for several years for construction of the new subway. This took away the open space that had been vital to residents of the over-crowded apartments nearby. The poor economy, the subway construction, the park closure, the overcrowded streets, the drugs, and the homeless all contributed to a large number of businesses closing. Some of these had been in the area for generations.

The MacArthur Park area does not fit the popular view of Los Angeles. It is dense and centralized rather than sprawling and unfocused; it is oriented toward the pedestrian rather than the car; it is hilly, not flat; and it has a good stock of traditional architecture, not just new strip malls. Many of its residents use public transportation, traveling to all parts of the city for work, while others stay almost entirely within the neighborhood. The sidewalks are filled with shoppers. Only the Broadway district in downtown Los Angeles is busier with everyday pedestrian activity. Vendors line the streets, selling

mangoes, perfume, magazines, cigarettes, tapes, roasted corn on sticks, socks, tamales, and much more. The streets resemble a bustling open-air market south of the border. Shoppers can get whatever they need, from green chiles to green cards.

In cities around the world, streets are full of vendors, but in Los Angeles, to vend is to break the law. Lookouts vigilantly watch for police, and vendors have clever ways of nonchalantly covering their goods or quickly packing up and moving, but most are regularly cited, arrested, or otherwise harassed by the police while the crack trade continues unabated nearby.[1] In spite of the threat of a misdemeanor arrest and a thousand-dollar fine, for many vending is the only option, the only means of immediate economic survival.[2]

Despite the fact that many are undocumented immigrants and therefore doubly vulnerable to legal troubles, over the last few years vendors have consolidated themselves into advocacy groups such as AVA (Asociación de los Vendedores Ambulantes) and SVCLA (Sidewalk Vending

Coalition of Los Angeles). With such outside organizations as CARECEN (Central American Resource Center), they began to question the prohibition formally and lobby the city council for the legalization of street vending. After a difficult political battle, the city council in 1994 passed an ordinance legalizing street vending for a two-year test period.[3] The ordinance stipulated the following strict guidelines for the experiment:

1. All legal vending is to be in specific districts (usually no larger than two or three square blocks), each with its own community-based administrative organization to manage vending in the district.

2. Each district will have specific boundaries and a specified number of vending spots, each to be permanently assigned to a single vendor.

3. Approval signatures of a significant percentage of business owners within the district are required in order to establish the district.

4. All vending is to be from approved mobile carts no larger than three feet six inches in width, six feet in length, and six feet in height. Vending cannot be conducted from shopping carts or plastic milk crates, and merchandise may not be placed on the sidewalk.

5. All food is to be prepared in vending kitchens administered by the district board.

6. All vendors must pay an annual licensing

1
Betty Jane Levine, "Of Carts and Corners," LOS ANGELES TIMES, January 26, 1992.

2
Jake Doherty, "Street Vendors Claim Police Harassment," LOS ANGELES TIMES, May 22, 1992.

3
James Rainey, "Vendors Cheer as Legalization Wins Final OK," LOS ANGELES TIMES, January 5, 1994.

fee and wear a vendor's badge at all times. **7.** Vending spots must keep a specified distance from corners, curbs, storefronts, and other vendors.[4]

Even though in 1994 the ordinance was not in effect, some vending advocates argued that the guidelines were too restrictive, laced with political and bureaucratic red tape that presented significant obstacles to the administration of the districts. They claimed that the majority of vendors would continue to vend illegally, thus dooming the experiment to failure. Others said that the ordinance was the first step in implementing legal vending in Los Angeles and anticipated that the districts would be expanded and the guidelines modified over time.

During the years before the ordinance passed, I began to take a personal interest in the plight of the MacArthur Park street vendors. I had lived and worked out of a studio overlooking the park for several years and found the neighborhood to be richly urban and ethnically fascinating. The thriving sidewalks around the park turned daily errands into a colorful journey of the senses as I passed through the bazaarlike atmosphere that seemed both un-American and yet so truly American.

In a democratic society, the street is a potent symbol of the public realm. I like the way vendors add character to the street environment and enhance the pedestrian experience. I feel the opportunity to use the public realm to sell what one has should be an unquestioned right. Vending on the street is a way to start with very little and build a business. Since most of Los Angeles vendors are Central Americans or African Americans, it might be argued that the antivending stance is racist. Nevertheless, the concerns of the store owners should not be overlooked. Their overhead costs make it difficult to compete with the vendor's prices. Some also argue that the vendor presence on the sidewalk impedes access to their stores. The health department has legitimate safety concerns. The city also needs to collect sales taxes. However, antivending policies effectively keep economically weak sectors of the population from getting stronger.

SERVICE STATION STUDIO

I began working with the vending community before the ordinance passed, through my work with the Service Station Studio. In 1992 I had collaborated with architect Chris Jarrett to organize the studio at the University of Southern California School of Architecture.[5] The studio grew out of debates with faculty members over the relative importance of social issues versus formal and theoretical ones in architecture and design. Chris and I argued that focusing on the latter to the exclusion of the former would isolate young architects from the contemporary city. Instead, we wanted to

4
Paraphrased from Los Angeles, California, Street Vending Ordinance, Administrative Code (January 1994).

5
I am indebted to my colleague and friend Chris Jarrett for his collaboration on many of the ideas expressed in this essay.

redefine the relationship between architectural education and the everyday city—the commonplace, repetitive activities of urban residents. We wanted to base the Service Station Studio on collaboration, on a dialogue between the conventions of architecture and the practices of everyday life.

We were also motivated by a belief that the civic infrastructure of Los Angeles was in decay, providing few services to city residents. We had many ideas for how these failures might be addressed, and our first project involved the decentralization of social services from the downtown civic center into individual neighborhoods. We felt this shift would improve access, increase use, and reduce costs. With a class of students, we began by studying various target issues of social services—crime, literacy, pregnancy, hunger, AIDS, and gangs. We also looked for heavily trafficked areas that might be prime locations for convenient distribution of services and determined that intersections with three or more mini-malls were the best candidates. Our concluding proposal entailed the reconstruction of the mini-malls and the installation of small "service stations," booths staffed by social-service professionals who could answer questions, offer literature, and direct clients to appropriate assistance or resources. A week before we were to begin attempting to implement the plan, the Rodney King verdict was announced and the city erupted. Most of the mini-malls with which we had planned to work burned down, tragically highlighting the enormous level of social dissatisfaction within the city and confirming the relevance of the issues we had explored. University officials and the local press praised the Service Station Studio, but we realized the work of the class still suffered from being too abstract, too strategic, and too far from the street.

L.A. SERVICE STATION PROJECT

In an effort to make the Service Station Studio less top-down and more tactical, Chris Jarrett and I organized an exhibition at the Los Angeles Municipal Art Gallery. It was this project that would formally involve me in the vending community. We asked a diverse group of architects to collaborate with local interest groups to develop modestly scaled, lightweight, affordable, and appropriate architectural prototypes that might improve life in Los Angeles. The eleven projects spanned the city, addressing ordinary but unnoticed places that outsiders often feared or mistakenly characterized as marginal. Although poor, the neighborhoods were actually rich in urban culture, shaped by local ritual, need, and ingenuity. Among the groups collaborating with the project's architects were itinerant construction laborers, garment workers, homeless people, schoolchildren, senior citizens, and street vendors. Each project was given a name ending in "station" that was intended to describe its purpose or activity (for example, the After School Station, the Training, Borrowing, and Repair Station, or the Community Information Station).

VENDING, WAITING, AND LOOKING STATION

Architect Barbara Bestor and I headed up a team that worked with street vendors, shop owners, shoppers, and young people around MacArthur Park called the Vending, Waiting, and Looking Station. Circumstantial and cluttered, the daily dynamics between curbside vendors, sidewalk musicians, corner preachers, loud radios, and bilingual store signage provided a self-made urbanism with which we, as designers, couldn't compete even if we wanted to. Our team met with the vending advocates at AVA and CARECEN, and we spent time hanging out and talking with street vendors and shop owners. We carefully scrutinized the proposed vending ordinance (it hadn't yet passed). We met Alberto Galica, a wheel-chair-bound street vendor who sells perfume on the sidewalk. Under the ordinance's guidelines, he would never be able to sell his perfume legally because it is impossible for him to push or pull a cart.

We decided to take the ordinance guidelines as our framework but also sought to examine and address the spectrum of vending practices that fell outside those parameters. We thought about ways to utilize sidewalks and unused spaces without infringing on the selling arenas of local merchants and property owners, but also assumed that a thriving street marketplace would lead to an overall increase in pedestrian traffic with a consequent increase in business for everyone.

With these goals in mind, we proposed to inhabit sidewalks and empty spaces with a mix of permanent, semipermanent, and supermobile structures. The empty lots and the nearby Metro Rail plaza, under construction at the time, had already been earmarked for grander designs, but we suggested that they be used in the interim for basketball, vending, and sitting in the shade. Like clothing, the layers of street structures could be expanded or removed as the neighborhood and the city changed. Of these projects, only two would satisfy the legal requirements of the new ordinance.

The Service Station exhibit helped spread ideas about street vending to a larger portion of the general public and also showed street vendors, shop owners, and politicians what could be possible.[6] As we met more vendors, advocates, and politicians, I was asked to become an advisory member of the Sidewalk Vending Coalition of Los Angeles. The SVCLA wanted to administer all eight of the ordinance's vending districts and had just initiated its PASEO project (Pedestrian Areas for Shopping and Economic Opportunity), which was self-described as a plan to "enhance neighborhood commercial corridors with color and charm [with the intention of] attacking blight and catalyzing economic growth."[7] With some hesitation, I agreed to get involved. I felt PASEO ran the risk of transforming these districts—areas that already had their own charm, color, and economic vitality—into small-scale clones of theme parks or shopping malls.

CART PROTOTYPES

During the summer of 1995, the SVCLA asked me to help create prototypes of vending carts for the new districts. Artist Gale McCall and I worked with students in the Insurgent Urbanism Studio at the Southern California Institute of Architecture (SCI-Arc) to design and build several models that would satisfy both the new ordinance and the vendors' needs. For their preliminary research, students visited vending districts, talked to vendors, advocates, and food-cart manufacturers, and learned to weld. The students collaboratively combined their individual designs to fabricate three prototypes out of steel, wood, rubber, and canvas. The carts were outfitted to accommodate the sale of fruit, clothes, or packaged goods, and were produced at a cost of $250 to $400 each.

The finished prototypes were displayed in several of the districts and were scrutinized by local vendors. They liked the carts, which also attracted the attention of the local press, but more importantly, they suggested ways to improve the designs.[8] Curiously, we were contacted by the developers of Universal Studio's Citywalk, who wanted to buy them for use in shopping malls across the country—exactly the effect we were trying to avoid. Our intention to produce the carts affordably in manufac-

6
An economic development initiative sponsored by the Sidewalk Vending Coalition of Los Angeles submitted on February 7, 1995, to the city of Los Angeles, Community Development Department. Written by Alison Leigh Becker, Ezekiel Mobley, and Jorge Sanchez on behalf of SVCLA.

7
Leon Whiteson, "Los Angeles Exhibit Proposes Small-Scale Urban Remedies," ARCHITECTURE, July 1994.

8
Maki Becker, "Street Vendors Appear to Be Sold on Budding Designers' Change of Cart," LOS ANGELES TIMES, November 10, 1995.

9
Stephanie Simon,
"MacArthur Park
OK'd as Special
Vending District,"
LOS ANGELES TIMES,
November 9, 1995.

turing runs of one hundred to two hundred was bogged down by lack of funding and by the stalemate in implementing the districts. Since we felt our work had failed, we gave the clothing cart to Wajeha Bilal, a vending advocate in Watts, and sold the other two to the Los Angeles Municipal Art Gallery, which would put them on display.

The carts would nonetheless have one more role to play in the ongoing vending controversy. In the fall of 1995, Jorge Perez of CARECEN approached me for assistance in finally getting official approval for MacArthur Park's vending district. He needed renderings to show the city council what the vending district would actually look like. Latino students at SCI-Arc had just formed SCI-udad (*ciudad* means "city" in Spanish) to promote Latino issues and involve the Latino community in architectural work, and they helped Perez by developing some amusing photocollages that inserted images of the SCI-Arc vending carts into MacArthur Park. In late 1995, the MacArthur Park area was designated as a legal vending district, the first in Los Angeles.[9]

ONGOING POLITICS

More than four years since the passage of the vending ordinance, and two years since the authorization of the MacArthur Park district, there is still no legal street vending in Los Angeles. The police department continues to cite, fine, and arrest vendors, and vendors continue to demand their rights. Most of the problems are political. Though the city council did indeed approve the vending district in MacArthur Park, the district advisory board—which consists of representatives from the local councilman's office and the Los Angeles Police Department as well as residents, business owners, and street vendors—has been unable to resolve the necessary administrative issues. For example, the board issued a request for proposals in search of an organization to manage the district; no one applied.

When or if legal vending gets under way in MacArthur Park, it is likely that much of the vending will still be illegal due to the unrealistic constraints of the ordinance. Requirements for food carts include such expensive accommodations as refrigeration and running water, a financial impossibility for most food vendors. The most lucrative vending items are currently cigarettes and bootleg audiotapes and compact disks. These will still, of course, be illegal under the new ordinance, but there will nonetheless always be a demand, and therefore probably a supply. Approximately 60 to 75 vendors now work in the MacArthur Park area during the week, and 80 to 120 on the weekends. The new district will only issue permits for 38 official spots, which means that most of the vendors will be forced to continue selling without authorization.[10] Finally, 18 of the 38 licensed vending spots have been set aside to sell arts and crafts, for no discernable reason. No one currently sells arts and crafts in the area—most of the vended items are daily necessities. As a consequence of this designation, almost half of the authorized vending spots will be used by vendors new to the area, further limiting opportunities for those now selling on the streets.

10
"Vendors Stage Protest Outside Police Station," LOS ANGELES TIMES, December 9, 1995.

11
Michel de Certeau, THE PRACTICE OF EVERYDAY LIFE (Berkeley and Los Angeles: University of California Press, 1988), 29.

ALTERNATIVE APPROACHES

While still willing to administer the districts, SVCLA and CARECEN are also looking for other ways in which the street vendors might operate legally. The SVCLA is negotiating with two private landowners to allow vending on their vacant lots. These locations are near MacArthur Park and could absorb some of the excess vending from that area. The SVCLA has also persuaded the Metropolitan Transit Authority to allow twenty or more permanent vending spots at the new Metro Rail stations in MacArthur Park and at the nearby intersection of Vermont Avenue and Wilshire Boulevard.

CARECEN and SVCLA are working with local economic-development groups to manufacture vending carts for these areas. In the summer of 1996, once again, they approached me for help. After they modify the SCI-Arc cart designs so they can be produced by fabricators in the MacArthur Park area, the groups will create master plans for vending layouts and landscape improvements in all of the Los Angeles vending sites.

As I continue to work with the vendors, I find that the carts have evolved in response to the tactics of daily opportunity. As Michel de Certeau said about urban tactics, "Sly as a fox and twice as quick. You see your opportunity and you take it."[11] We have learned to make the carts opportunistic. While the basic models adhere closely to the proscriptions of the vending ordinance, they are designed to be expanded or contracted beyond those limits at a moment's notice to serve the real everyday needs of Los Angeles street vendors.

The ongoing efforts toward legitimizing street vending remain open-ended and inconclusive, punctuated by small victories and defeats. In this indefinite battle lies a lesson about how architects can most effectively approach working in the realm of the everyday city. The everyday city is about the struggle for survival and the attendant blurring of the economic, the social, and the domestic. Architects who involve themselves beyond structures and aesthetics do so because they want to make the community a bit better, but they must be willing to work within a painstakingly gradual process. Projects of the everyday city don't fit into existing schedules, particularly those of professional designs or school semesters. Instead they have a character more like that of the city itself, with lifetimes and momentums of their own. This can be difficult for those who interact with this realm; the mundane qualities of this work frequently lead to ambivalence and exhaustion. I have come to realize, however, that these two states may compromise the very essence of the everyday.

Ambivalence entails the simultaneous embrace of opposing feelings about a specific issue. This condition is essential to the quality of open-mindedness that brings about change for the better and can lead to action that is guided not by doctrine but by attentiveness to the specific day-to-day situations. Resulting decisions are more tactically responsive than strategically pre-determined. Intermittent exhaustion helps to establish a repetitive pattern of work and rejuvenation, culminating in either an attitude of optimism or futility. Such a great amount of effort followed by so little, or such slow progress tends to be frustrating and unsatisfying and often leads to giving up this sort of work. As the I Ching tells us, "Gradual progress is the most enduring." Belief in this tenet has allowed me to maintain a positive outlook in spite of sporadic progress. After a big push, these projects often go into hibernation until the next budget, the next election, or the next media blitz. But after a rest, the work always rears its ugly, or beautiful, head again. I approach it slowly, amazed that it is still alive. It is precisely because it is alive that I give it another hand.

L.A. SERVICE STATION PROJECT 1994:
VENDING, WAITING, AND LOOKING STATION DRAWINGS

Projects by Norman Millar, Barbara Bestor, Thurman Grant, Gale McCall, Celia Miller, Hoa Trinh

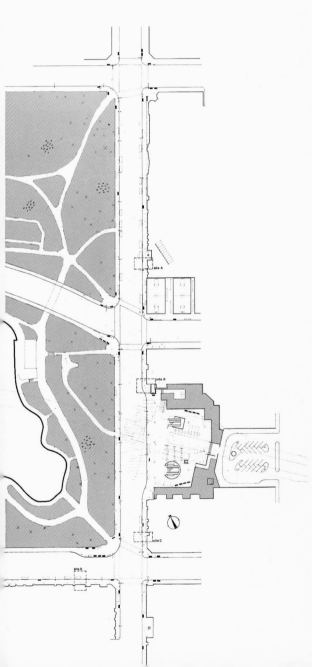

PERMANENTS
(Infrastructural elements with
community-based ornament)

Site Plan shows the east end of MacArthur Park, with proposed sidewalk improvements as well as prospective locations for Permanents, Semipermanents, and Supermobiles.

Sidewalk Pavers demarcate vending spaces for carts and will be customized in workshops with neighborhood children. More permanent than mural art and graffiti, this layer of infrastructure can be created in cooperation with local youth organizations to establish a community identity. With the pavers, the sidewalk will look somewhat like Hollywood's Walk of Stars, but less predictable.

Waiting Walls provide a place for leaning and resting and can be accessorized with shade structures, customized countertops, and shelves. They can also be used as immobile vending stations for the disabled. These corrugated-concrete structures, thirty-two inches in height with varying widths, will be located on sidewalks along curbs as well as within the open-lot marketplaces.

SUPERMOBILES
(Very easy to set up or roll away)

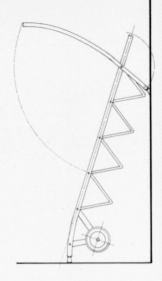

Lean-To Walls function like Lean-to Cars but are slightly larger, are supported by walls, and have wheels. Like loading dollies, they can be rolled to and from any available wall space.

Lean-To Cars are shelving units for displaying merchandise. They incorporate a shallow roof for shade and lean against a car for support. Their compact design allows for transport in or on their proprietors' cars.

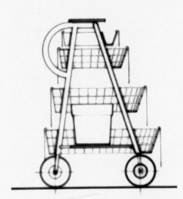

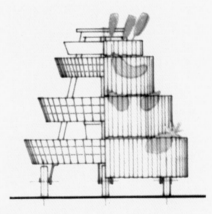

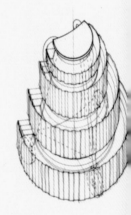

Fruit Ziggurats are small, wheeled display carts intended for the vending of more fanciful goods. Inspired by the stylized cutting and showcasing of mangoes and other ready-to-eat fruits, the Ziggurats maximize display area with concentric semicircular shelves.

SEMIPERMANENTS
(Mobile units for assigned spaces
to be used by licensed vendors)

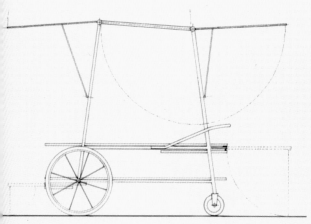

Go-Carts are built using bicycle technology. They are lightweight but very sturdy, consisting of an affordable basic model that can be accessorized with hanging frameworks and roof structures. The Sidewalk Pavers will indicate the Go-Carts' licensed vending spots. When not in use proprietors can roll their carts to a parking structure.

Pivot Posts are devices from which vendors can hang merchandise. Hinged beams affixed to designated wall surfaces, the Pivot Posts unfold to be perpendicular to the wall. They will be mounted high enough to allow pedestrians to walk under and around the hanging merchandise.

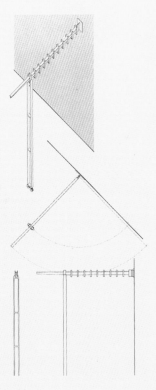

WALTER HOOD

URBAN DIARIES:
IMPROVISATION
IN
WEST OAKLAND,
CALIFORNIA

PHOTOGRAPHS BY LEW WATTS

In contrast to the standard design models usually applied to the "improvement" of low-income areas, a new method, "improvisation," can help to transform real social and cultural patterns into physical form. Improvisation begins by documenting these patterns in particular neighborhoods. Understanding everyday activities forces the designer to confront a neighborhood's dynamic economic, physical, and social structures. This comprehension creates a direct link between planning and true-to-life community issues, fully incorporating the human condition into the design process. Both objective and interpretive, consisting of both commentary and research, the improvisation process illuminates particular attitudes about place and culture from a point of view that is simultaneously inside and outside. Posing hard questions, the designer confronts the real issues that face our urban communities. Improvisational design strategies make these indigenous patterns and issues visible to the neighborhood and to outsiders, which allows the residents and their daily lives to shape their own communities. This essay focuses on the planning and design process of a West Oakland minipark but could apply equally to many inner-city neighborhoods in the United States.

MODEL CITIES AND MINIPARKS

The Model Cities Program, highly praised by planners in the late 1960s, was created to help improve the physical and social environment of "blighted" portions of major American cities. The program's predominant goal was "slum eradication." The neighborhood of West Oakland in Northern California was placed under the Model Cities auspices in 1970. Amid considerable fanfare, broad swaths of the targeted neighborhoods were demolished to make way for blocks of new low-income housing, neighborhood parks, and open space. Revisiting West Oakland today, Model Cities solutions are still in evidence. Yet, twenty-five years after its reconfiguration as a Model Cities neighborhood, the community has once again been designated as "blighted" by the Oakland City Planning Department, newly ripe for redevelopment. The parks, open spaces, and housing projects created under the Model Cities Program have become public nuisances: turf for illicit activity and ongoing vandalism. Parasite enterprises such as liquor stores, check-cashing establishments, and fast-food restaurants have proliferated. Promised economic programs have never materialized, and the transportation infrastructure has bypassed the community, further isolating it from the central city. These are mean landscapes.

The urban minipark, now common in many inner-city neighborhoods, was a key element of the Model Cities redevelopment programs. Planners and advocates saw miniparks as a valuable commodity, a pragmatic extension of the open-space movement's scramble to create parklands in cities. Competition for land, particularly with freeways and housing, was greater than ever before, so open-space ideology rationalized the minipark, the play lot, and the vest-pocket park, small parks that could be tucked into irregular, unusual, inexpensive sites that had been rejected in prior eras.[1]

Urban miniparks exist in most American cities, and their form and design are remarkably consistent: an open green area, serpentine in form, with standardized amenities such as manufactured play environments, benches, game tables, drinking fountains, and, occasionally, court areas for such sports as basketball, handball, and tetherball. Embedded in these standard and programmatic elements are strategies of social reform that allow only normative or mainstream use of the spaces.

The urban minipark is a space that many people pass every day. Adults or older siblings bring small children to play at the park. Groups of school-age children may briefly stop in the park en route to other places in the neighborhood. Teens with no other place to go might perch on the minipark's benches, scoping the street. On a warm evening, a pickup game of half-court basketball sometimes enlivens the park. The minipark is a structured environment, programmed for specific groups of people and recreational activities.

Other people use the urban minipark, but their needs subvert the original goals of site. We see these activities every day: homeless adults enjoying conversation and a drink, neighborhood recyclers pushing their shopping carts into the park to rest for a bit, teenagers expressing themselves through tagging and graffiti. The minipark formula leaves these disenfranchised members of society without a sense of legitimate right to use the space. Social injustices are created when certain needs are ignored and unaccommodated in the park's initial planning and design, and conflicts arise when unprogrammed uses occur.

These clashes between programmed and unprogrammed uses of community facilities raise critical questions for designers, particularly in urban neighborhoods. As public space becomes scarce in an increasingly privatized urban environment, and as the budgets of public agencies dwindle, how can amenities such as these miniparks be redesigned to serve the community more effectively? The values and attitudes that have shaped these spaces have historically been derived from middle-class values, an outsider's viewpoint. What methods would better allow the voices within the communi-

1
Galen Cranz, THE POLITICS OF PARK DESIGN (Cambridge, Mass.: MIT Press, 1986), 147.

2
Randolph Hester,
PLANNING
NEIGHBORHOOD
SPACE (New York:
Van Nostrand
Reinhold, 1984),
117.

ty to be heard? If designers were to re-cre-ate public spaces according to the actual practices and familiar patterns of neighbor-hood residents, would a different set of values, attitudes, and forms unfold? And perhaps the most fundamental question, shouldn't people be entitled to public spaces in their neighborhoods that meet their needs?

URBAN OBSERVATION

The theoretical reconfiguration of a mid-block urban minipark in West Oakland reveals the ways in which improvisational design can open up new levels of communi-ty awareness and empowerment, and offers a pragmatic illustration of how disenfran-chised communities can participate in reconstructing their public environment. This park, initially developed as a clean, defin-able package embracing mainstream American ideals about open space, does not reflect the unique qualities and needs of the neighborhood it serves. Throwing away preconceived notions, moral stances, and reformist approaches, the improvisational process juxtaposes an awareness of history with the observation of rhythms of every-day life, allowing the designer's eyes and ears to open up to the community. Histori-cal research is familiar to most designers; examination of everyday life is not. Yet as landscape architect Randolph Hester writes, observation "is the single best technique for discovering what people do and how people interact with other people in neighborhood space."[2] This urban diary structures the observations I have made over the course of a year in West Oakland. Witnessed and documented, scenarios of everyday experience construct new narra-tives: the old men sitting in the park telling stories, the unattended children of single mothers who have no time to take them to the park, the entrepreneurial activity of automobile detailing at the park's periphery, and the daily routines of local prostitutes. Each activity, event, or circumstance sug-gests a major theme for investigation. A multitude of voices can be heard, some that had the ear of park planners twenty years ago and others that—then, as now—we ignore because we do not want to hear.

DURANT MINIPARK

Durant Minipark sits on a quarter-acre lot where a house once stood, sandwiched between an elementary school and a pair of duplexes. Only the front edge of the space is open to the street. The block is mostly residential, with single-family houses, apart-ments, rooming houses, and artists' studios. A liquor and grocery store on the corner and an adjacent four-lane street are within walking distance. The park includes hardy eucalyptus trees and evergreen shrubs, manufactured play equipment, game tables, benches, and a drinking fountain.

Durant Minipark

The park is usually vacant for most of the day. Apart from those stopping to drink on their way back from the corner store, the space has very few users. The play equipment, benches, and drinking fountain sit in the park like ruins, weathered by time and neglect. Durant Minipark appears to have been placed in the community by foreign hands. In contrast, the adjacent large grounds of Durant School overflow with local kids, who play basketball, baseball, and tag, run track, or simply hang out, all whether or not school is in session.

Responding to the various voices and needs of the community, a designer can, using improvisational methods, transform the midblock park from unused oddity to neighborhood amenity. When applied to urban planning and design, improvisation— in its generic meaning, creating, fabricating, and composing using what is at hand—is a method of reshaping a particular environment based on preexisting local resources, inspirations, and opportunities. The following theoretical transformations of Durant Minipark build on journal entries documenting the everyday patterns and practices of the neighborhood. Improvisations take their cue from these actions and events, guiding change from within the neighborhood.

An open mind is the key to understanding difference as documented here. No attempts have been made to conform to institutional policies or political positions.

The neighborhood—one previously voiceless in determining how its own public spaces were designed—is now the client.

THE DIARIES

These diary entries consist of direct transcriptions of actual uses and observed events in Durant Minipark. The diary entries are divided into two sections, "The Park" and "The Street." Each section further breaks down into five days, with each day representing one layer of observation and analysis, showcasing one function and producing one new solution. Each day incorporates the following sections: Observation, Analysis, Solution, and Vision, the last illustrating a speculative glimpse at what the park might be with the respective innovation.

THE PARK
Day One
Observation: I've noticed this garden for a long time. Always neat. Vegetables and

roses commingled, creating beautiful borders along the sidewalk. Multicolored plants playfully contrast with the green lawn. I've always been intrigued by the water jugs along the path. Why are they there? My barber tells me they keep dogs out. I've never seen the gardener, but when I do, I'll ask him or her about the jugs.

Analysis and Solution: The garden, a place of intense horticultural activity, is the first layer. Raised planting beds are situated to take advantage of the sun, and grids of fruit trees face each other, flanking a path to the garden shed. Herbs proliferate along the garden's edge. The initial framework is the golden section, the primary ordering system for spatial patterns in the garden. The primary requirements for the garden are human access and agricultural output sufficient for a minimum of ten families—one half of the block's population. The garden needs a mere six thousand square feet, a low number perhaps because not all of the

residents on the street participate in the ritual of gardening. Horticulturist Bruce Stokes estimates that a family of four can produce two-thirds of its vegetables on six hundred square feet of land with five hours of cultivation time per week.[3] On the first day, this is the garden's only use. The first layer of use is one-dimensional: neighborhood residents growing their own vegetables.

Vision: I never see more than one or two people in the garden at any given time, but the plentiful bounty reveals their labor and dedication. Corn, collard greens, potatoes, and flowers are densely planted in the raised beds. Neighborhood kids have turned the storage shed into a playhouse. When the gardeners leave, the children play tag and hide-and-seek among the vegetable beds.

From Day One, the garden accepts the local children and functions as their playground. The children are allowed to inhabit the garden shed, and it becomes a clubhouse. The children's imagination trans-

3
Bruce Stokes,
HELPING OURSELVES:
LOCAL SOLUTIONS TO
GLOBAL PROBLEMS
(New York: W. W.
Norton, 1981), 48.

Day One: Neighborhood and the garden

forms the structure into a starship, a fort, and so on. A sandbox sits nearby and accommodates imaginative play. These elements serve as a starting point for investigating Durant Minipark's play environment for children.

Day Two

Observation: The kids never play on the play equipment. When I pass by, I see them digging in the dirt or climbing the old sycamore tree. The chain-link fence has become a wavemaker, and the sandbox wall is the forum for Simon Says games. They never use the play equipment, or at least I don't see them using it.

Analysis and Solution: Based on these observations, I have eliminated playground equipment from my theoretical redesign due to limited use patterns and safety considerations. Designer Mark Rios argues that a typical prefabricated play apparatus "dictates a certain way to use it, which is climbing. But developing physical skills accounts for only ten percent of all activity at the playground."[4] In this second layer of examination, children are seen as adven-

turous, curious, and imaginative. They play games in various spaces and on various surfaces: turf, sand, asphalt, concrete, and decomposed granite. The multiple environments sponsor diversity of play, learning, and new experience. The sandbox is the only feature I would not change—it is a popular place for the smaller tots to mold and build under the watchful eyes of guardians. The play yard without equipment will allow children to invent and create their own connections between objects and environment.

Vision: Two girls have a tea party on the sloping grass plane. They turn the tool shed into a playhouse, pretending it is their home. The two girls yell at their brothers, who are busy playing something like tag, cops-and-robbers, and hide-and-seek all rolled into one. In the sandbox, two kids build a castle with tools borrowed from the

4
Mark Rios, "Redefining the Idea of Play," LANDSCAPE ARCHI-TECTURE, February 1994, 72.

Day Two: Playhouse

gardeners. Their activities transform the whole scene into a playhouse.

Day Three

Observation: Spring brings out the gazanias and the lovers. With their bottles of Olde English from the corner store, they sit at the picnic table, and maybe don't even talk. They sit there together. They watch the street, together.

Analysis and Solution: The third transformation begins with a metaphorical construct, the lovers. The space becomes a backdrop for the development of human relationships. The lovers flock to a perch that looms high above the park. A place for couples, friends, or the weary, the perch sets its occupants apart from the other activities at ground level. This is a familiar place for those who want privacy—but who also want to be seen. The perch is a basic construction, a balloon-frame structure with a simple double-gable metal roof. Railings and stairs offer safety and access. Fruit blossoms, sage, and a blue aura permeate the space.

This is a place for encounters, conversations, and love.

Vision: They come to sit together, whether at street level or in the tower rising above the neighborhood. Accentuated by isolation and solidarity, their intimacy becomes more powerful. Their couple-ness is visible to the street. Looking out on the street, they are there to be seen. They have a space of their own, together, as long as this sunset lasts.

Day Four

Observation: Brown paper bag in hand, they leave the store and head straight for the park. It is the stopping point for drinking a beer and taking in the sights along the street. A picnic table and two benches are the only seats. Once the beer is consumed, they go on their way.

Analysis: The consumption of alcoholic beverages on public grounds is currently prohibited, but the rule is consistently ignored and unenforced. In further contradiction to the ban, the sale of beer is the number-one source of revenue for neighborhood merchants. The popularity

Day Three: The perch

of twenty-two and forty-ounce bottles of malt liquor—more malt liquor for less money—in marginal ethnic communities is a marketing coup for beer distributors and corporations.

Solution: These now illicit activities turn my thoughts to the beer gardens of Munich and, even closer to home, the occasional beer a homeowner might have after mowing the lawn on a warm afternoon. The beer-garden model is a simple program that could inform a solution. In Durant Minipark, the beer garden would not be a place for beer sales but a space to sit and relax where beer consumption was not pro-hibited. Rows of trees, seating, a cultivated garden, and shelter from the street would all welcome the beer drinker. The familiar in this case is disguised under the gesture of inclusion—allowing the practices to continue.

Vision: Rows of seats in the beer garden are filled on a hot day. Bags in hand, they all share stories and a laugh or two. The beer drinkers that want to be seen sit on the porch. Others sit toward the back, lounging and watching the gardeners, the lovers, and the playing children.

Day Five

Observation: I had to pull the car over to let them by. Shopping carts banging against one another—the sound of glass is musical, like that of a chandelier near an open win-

Day Four: Beer garden

dow. One guides from the front; the other pushes mechanically from the back. Like a train, the carts and their conductors plod down the center of the street. In a choreographed dance, the one in the rear casually slips away, returning with prizes scooped from Gertrude's trash. Pulling and pushing, they continue down the center of the street oblivious to the cars maneuvering around them. That night, I awake to a mysterious rattle and peer at the clock, which reads 3:00 AM. A distant rattle grows to a clang and then a beautiful chorus of tinkles. I turn over and resume my sleep—the chorus slips past. Bottles fill my dreams. In the morning, the bag of empty beer bottles I'd left by the door has vanished.

Analysis: This concept is antithetical to the city's recycling program, which refuses the cart people's collections.

Solution: A recycling structure will allow residents to bring their recycling materials to the park; wide enough for shopping carts to roll through, the structure will allow those who collect cans and bottles along the street to come and retrieve items on a daily basis. Recycling expands the structure's meaning and use: it can be used simultaneously as a utility room, recycling shed, and whatever the children imagine it to be.

Vision: They are always there first thing in the morning to clean out the bright yellow city-issue recycling bins. I left mine there last night, a small batch of bottles. As if they are shopping in a grocery store, they steer their carts down the aisles, sorting bottles and cans for carting to the recycling center. Other collectors are too late—the recycling shed has been cleared. I return after work to get my empty yellow bin.

THE IMPROVISATIONAL DURANT MINIPARK

The vegetable plants and their accoutrements expand along the eastern boundary of the park. Salvia and lavender

Day Five: Recycling bins

borders lace the bottom of the evergreen hedges that enclose the beer garden's seating spaces. An allée of fruit trees marches along the western boundary. The sandbox is tucked between stands of bamboo at the rear of the site. The perch is expanded to encompass two rooms next to the street. The multiuse structure bustles with playing children, working gardeners, and industrious recyclers. Set together in a beautiful composition, the garden, sandbox, perch, beer seating, and recycling facilities have transformed the park's space into a unique and particular place. No single programmatic piece dominates the space—the ethos of difference and inclusion creates a place with multiple meanings, one that underscores many neighborhood practices at odds with normative societal values and attitudes.

THE STREET

It becomes clear that neighborhood residents use the street along and around the park as open space more than they use the park itself. According to Jane Jacobs: "The more successfully a city mingles everyday diversity of uses and users in its everyday streets, the more successfully, casually (and economically) its people thereby enliven and support well-located parks that can thus give back grace and delight to their neighborhoods instead of vacuity."[5]

The incorporation of design interventions in, and between, both park and street responds to the life and time of the neighborhood environment, creating a diversity of interpretations and uses for public space. So the street's pulse of activity guides a second set of diaries.

Day One

Observation: Simultaneous images of Oprah Winfrey project onto the street from three color televisions. Two tables, a recliner, and a broken lamp complete the living-room ensemble on the lawn. A tall man is drinking a bumper of Olde English as two big guys unload a set of yard chairs from a truck. As Oprah goes to a commercial break, Johnny Gill kicks in from the stereo lodged in the upstairs window. Two cute girls emerge

5
Jane Jacobs, THE DEATH AND LIFE OF GREAT AMERICAN CITIES (New York: Random House, 1961), 84–86.

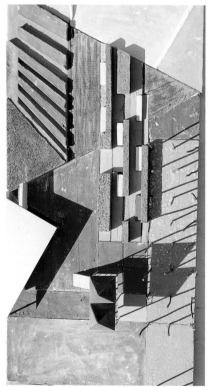

Final model of Durant Minipark

onto the street, busting a few new moves. Three naval cadets stop to purchase a chair. The scene is quite surreal: Johnny Gill and the feet and hands of the two girls. Buyers and sellers take over the street.

Analysis: The driveway runs along the edge of the single-family open lot, extending from the street to the back of the house. Once it may have culminated in a rear garage or carriage house, but today it leads to a concrete patio. The driveways are concrete floors, with dimensions dictated by automobile measurements—from ten to fifteen feet wide. On Twenty-ninth Street, cars are either parked in the driveway or along the curb for a quick and easy exit. The driveways accommodate auto repair, car washing, children's play, the depositing of collectible goods, or, occasionally, storing a boat that needs fixing. The driveway hosts many activities, from birthday parties to basketball games.

Solution: The residents of the houses on Twenty-ninth Street need a place to protect, display, and sell their collections. The selling block transfigures the driveway and provides a permanent proscenium for the residents' wares; they will no longer have to cart the goods on and off a truck for display on the lawn. The selling block is composed

Day One: Selling block

of five major elements: roof, floor, columns, wall, and ramp. Classically ordered, they create a side porch that faces the front yard. The blue wall, a stained stucco armature—firm, thick, and scaleless, a tribute to David Hockney's vision of California—is the block's signature. The fence wall and driveway are "environmental fortuna."[6] Constructed along the property line, the wall is simply a fence between neighbors, but by adding a floor, roof, and columns, storage opportunities unfold. The roof is constructed of brushed metal, reflecting the sky above and protecting the collectibles below. Connected to the fence wall and to the columns, the roof sheds water across the front and through a scupper on the wall side. The runoff will fall flush, sheeting down the front, then gush down a 45-degree "cut" into a ground-level drain. Six columns, tall and slender, march across the front, hoisting the roof upward. Centrally located at the front of the selling block, the ramp slips between two columns and slopes down to connect with the yard's central sidewalk. The selling block is raised on a concrete dock for easy loading and unloading.

Vision: Sitting tall and proud, the selling block has now replaced the driveway. The collectors have a place of business that keeps their collections dry, protected, and in full view of the street. With items neatly displayed against the wall, the stage is set for today's sales. The bargains and deals are ready to commence. First on the block: two color televisions and a Thonet chair. The truck backs up to the dock and unloads a brass bed. A customer rushes over to make her bid.

Day Two

Observation: Razor-sharp shadows cut across the asphalt as the sun sets on Twenty-ninth Street. Baby is strutting as boys and men rubberneck in her direction. Looking up and down the street, she adjusts the slit of her skirt to reveal a long white leg. Within minutes, a midnight blue Blazer cautiously motions by. Baby nods to the driver, all the while scanning the streets for detection. With a simple gesture, he attracts her and she hops into the open door. The journey is short—two hundred feet. The "date" itself is very quick—two or three minutes. He makes a sharp U-turn and drops her off at the place of origin. As she saunters back down the street, he takes one final look before driving away.

Analysis: Promiscuity, lust, and money are daily influences on the street. Street prostitution is usually closely associated with neighborhood blight. The right neighborhood, intersection, and street are central commercial considerations for streetwalkers; neighborhoods where apathy is high and police surveillance scarce are most preferred. Walking by dilapidated buildings, liquor stores, and apartment complexes, women of the street solicit all who pass

6
"Environmental fortuna," as formulated by Lars Lerup, suggests that "in order to know an object, we must embrace, study, all its sides. Once some or all of its sides are revealed, prompted, or discovered, the object is to reveal its opportunity." The blue wall thus becomes a receptacle, revealing its openness to improvisation. Lars Lerup, BUILDING THE UNFINISHED (Beverly Hills: Sage Publications, 1977), 129.

their way. The act of prostitution typically takes place within the confines of the client's automobile. The couple chooses a private place to park for the performance of services. Under the freeway, curbside next to vacant buildings, the automobile is the only buffer between the sex act and an audience of neighbors. In full view of passing children or the occasional glance from a nearby window, invisibility cloaks the auto and its occupants. In many cities, red-light districts are established to house certain darker sides of our desires, with institutions that cater to the needs of the lonely or sexually needy. Prostitution is featured in a blaze of lights and women. In America, prostitution is illegal in most states, but that does not make it go away, especially in blighted neighborhoods.

Solution: The drive-in brothel becomes a new institution on the neighborhood street. It shrouds the prostitute and the partner and, paradoxically, makes them visible in the community. The drive-in brothel's dimensions are familiar, governed by the shape and size of automobiles—like a parking space, the structure takes up residence at the curb. The roof and doors are the union of two circles, representing male and female. The lower circle is retractable and the upper is stationary. Once the car enters, the door lowers itself along an inside track. Operated with coins and dollar bills, the brothel garage offers five-,ten-, or fifteen-minute stays. Vending machines, stocked weekly with condoms, are prominently featured on the interior.

Vision: She accepts his nod and jumps in the front seat of the car. He is middle-aged and white; she is tall and black. They drive slowly as she discusses payment. Once at the booth, the car disappears. She drops the coins in and the doors come down. Fifteen minutes later, he is satisfied, and she is a little richer.

Day Two: Drive-in brothel

Day Three

Observation: The San Francisco 49ers are destroying the Dallas Cowboys. The Sunday football game on television turns out to be a drag for the six boys. They burst out the door onto the street. Football in hand, Nike Airs in the wind, the teams are chosen quickly, and the drive begins.

Analysis: As automobiles became inescapable fixtures in American cities, public officials and residents have struggled to reconcile the car and the social life of the street. In the late 1960s the closed street mall eliminated automobile traffic in downtown cores to accommodate pedestrians. But, rather than enhancing street life, this reduced social events to commercial activities. The residential version of this was the closed or slow street. This idea continues to seduce many neighborhoods into installing speed bumps or intersection barriers in order to slow cars down and deter traffic. But cars don't need to be banished. A vibrant street life is produced by the mixture of many diverse events and variables, including those generated by cars.

Donald Appleyard's seven characteristics of the ideal street set valuable standards for reclaimed and improved street life.[7] But Appleyard does not discuss how automobiles and the socializing that takes place in and around them might be incorporated into the ideal street. In working-class neighborhoods, the car is an indicator of social status—for many, the only capital investment a person will make—and therefore takes center stage for daily activities. Stopping and starting, newsing and tinkering, the car is a focus and priority.[8] The street should incorporate the familiar relationships that currently exist between people and their automobiles.

Solution: Twenty-ninth Street is a two-lane street with parking along both curbs. The stadium is established with three simple architectural gestures: stoop benches placed along the curb, tall poplar trees spaced regularly between the benches, French drains placed every ten yards to

Day Three: Street stadium

7
Appleyard's seven characteristics of the ideal street are: safe sanctuary; livable, healthy environment; community; neighborhood territory; place to play and learn; green and pleasant land; and unique historic place. Donald Appleyard, LIVABLE STREETS (Berkeley and Los Angeles: University of California Press, 1981), 243.

8
Paul Groth, "Vernacular Parks," in DENATURED VISIONS: LANDSCAPE AND CULTURE IN THE TWENTIETH CENTURY (New York: Museum of Modern Art, 1991).

drain the street across its crown.

Cars are still allowed on the street, but the drains slow the traffic. People gather to sit on the benches in the shade of the poplars as the football game begins. When there is no game on the street, cars can park next to the stoop benches. With open doors and loud music, the street becomes an extension of the car. Social gatherings, car upkeep, and other activities abound.

Vision: Moments after the big professional football game is over, the residents of the street take their seats to watch their own neighborhood game. Tall poplars shimmer like banners above a stadium as the game gets into gear. The street is alive with cheering.

Day Four

Observation: She seems lost as she prances back and forth, up and down the street. Dark shadows hide her face—bitter eyes

dance, subservient out of need. Like magic her appearance is quick. In a flash she has made a decision; she heads toward that familiar car, appearing and disappearing.

Analysis: The lack of affordable housing in American neighborhoods has reached alarming proportions. The lack of diversity in the housing market is particularly bleak, considering the changing demographics in urban neighborhoods. In this West Oakland neighborhood, as single-parent households, couples, the elderly, and the poor occupy housing designed for nuclear families, they transform these familiar structures.

Solution: A Baptist church's parking lot sits empty on most days of the week. On Sundays, the congregation gathers and later departs. An easement, fifteen feet wide along the lot's east edge, could be created to offer homes to local street prostitutes. The southern rural house type—the shot-

Day Three: Street stadium

gun house—here provides a familiar model for a new kind of seven-unit apartment building. The number seven is used for its sacred symbolism; it represents "the wholeness and completeness of all created things."[9] Stretching along the edge of the lot, units are stacked three stories high, one atop the other. A walled garden at the rear of the property provides a place for daily labor—toiling in the soil to renew the spirit—and a means of subsistence. The seven units share a common hall. At the complex's corners, stairs spiral up to the roof deck—a place to view the street and skyline. The western face of the building is pierced with windows, opposite the church for constant confrontations with the sacred. At sunset, evening shadows move across the front of the building to perish in the night.

Vision: Arriving home, she passes other studios before arriving at her own. The sun is bright as it sets over the bay. The church seems larger in its silhouette. As she undresses to shower, the shadow of the

steeple makes its way into her room. For a brief moment, she feels secure.

Day Five

Observation: Removing my shirt and stepping into the shower, I remember that the natural marbled cocoa-butter bar of soap disintegrated during my last shower. Turning the knob counterclockwise, I slip my shirt back on as the gushing water returns to its drip. Walking down to the corner store in the evening air briefly renews my energy. On the street, a hand beckons for change, but my gesture repels the exchange. Big Man is behind the counter at the store, his Islamic chants permeating the dark, dingy room. I circulate once and return to the counter. Big Man is busy with a shopper. Olde English, bologna, and three candy bars cross the counter between customer and owner. She is loud as she exclaims, "I'm short, you know I'm good." Big Man shrugs and bags her evening meal. With attentive eyes, he scans the store until I speak: "Do you have any soap?" Pointing to the far aisle, "Over

9
Lorna Price,
THE PLAN OF SAINT
GALL IN BRIEF
(Berkeley and Los
Angeles: University
of California Press,
1983), 28-30.

Day Four: Home for a prostitute

10
William Whyte,
THE SOCIAL LIFE OF
SMALL URBAN SPACES
(New York:
Doubleday, 1980),
57.

11
Kevin Lynch
defines imageabil-
ity as the "quality
in a physical
object that gives it
a high probability
of evoking a
strong image in
any given observ-
er. It is that
shape, color, or
arrangement that
facilitates the
making of vividly
identified, power-
fully structured,
highly useful men-
tal images of the
environment."
Kevin Lynch, THE
IMAGE OF THE CITY,
(Cambridge,
Mass.: MIT Press,
1960), 9.

there." I browse somberly and find only two standard brands—Ivory and Dial. I ponder for an eternity and return with the carefully chosen Ivory. My walk back to the counter takes me past a fully stocked cooler of malt liquor, two rows of standard canned and paper goods, and a barrage of candy and snack foods. Big Man rings up the Ivory and I pay. As the brown bag crosses between us, Big Man shrugs. We go through it once again, as we do every time I find myself in this store: I ask him why he is killing my people with such a selection of goods in his "grocery store." He looks at me with a resigned eye; it is as if he knows my people are doomed. As I step out into the dusk, his foreign chants reverberate over the street.

Analysis: When I was a child, my mother could telephone her orders to the neighbor-hood store and I would race a half mile to retrieve the groceries. A trip to the store meant two-for-one cookies and a white apron behind the butcher counter. Today commerce in this neighborhood is malt liquor and cigarettes. Businesses such as check-cashing facilities, liquor stores, and fast-food restaurants have come to feast. The neighborhood store benefits from the corporate propaganda that fills the visual landscape of the inner city. When I smoked, people would ask why I smoked Newports. "It was the only brand advertised in my neighborhood. The Marlboro Man never vis-

ited," I replied. The corner is a place to see and be seen. Next to the store, young and old stand around talking and watching the street. Every now and then someone will pull up in a car to stop and talk. Although William Whyte describes the corner as "a place for a great show" and a sign of vitali-ty and community spirit, in the inner city, congregating on corners usually implies illicit activities and trouble.[10]

Solution: The neighborhood store can spear-head change. The building is stripped bare and the transformation begins. The facade is broken open on the street side, bringing light into the small quarters. Changes in liquor licensing have forced merchants to use creative marketing. A deli goes in along the rear wall. The aisles are wider and the counter now looks out over the entire store. Vegetable bins are movable, indoors to out-doors. The corner has an awning and chairs, a place to stop and chat and hang out. At night the steel doors roll down. Next to the store, a market stall is set up with an over-look elevated high above the street, forming a new gateway. The overlook is an "image-able structure," providing the street with an identity that projects from the community to passersby.[11] Neighbors and merchants sell vegetables and other merchandise. The overlook is the nucleus of the street's neigh-borhood watch program—each neighbor regularly takes his or her turn in the watch-tower next to the corner store.

Vision: Big Man wakes up from his dream soaking wet, terrified by visions of his regular customers walking toward him, small brown bags in their outstretched hands, bodies gaunt and malnourished. They were all over him, silhouettes screaming "killer," faceless shadows. He awakens to his responsibility to this community in which he lives and works. The next day Big Man closes his store. Within a month, he reopens, offering five types of soap, fresh produce, a small deli. Two black faces can be seen standing behind the counter through the once boarded-up window.

It is Sarah's day to watch. She grabs her sketchbook and paints to pass the time; the watchtower is a great place to draw. She climbs the stairs and relieves the morning shift, Miss Mable, who tells Sarah about the day's events and a bit more before leaving. Sarah moves to her position, sketchbook in hand. She nods to a merchant below, confirming that stall three is available. She looks down the street and smiles at two kids who look up and say hello as they race to the store.

EPILOGUE

City parks are not abstractions, or automatic repositories of virtue or uplift, anymore than sidewalks are abstractions. They mean nothing divorced from their practical, tangible uses, and hence they mean nothing divorced from the tangible effects on them—for good or ill—of the city districts and uses touching them.

—Jane Jacobs,
The Death and Life of
Great American Cities

These diaries present a wide variety of human experiences, suggesting equally diverse possibilities for changes to West Oakland's Durant Minipark and its surroundings. The entries present one way to listen to the stories and lives of neighborhood residents, one way to see the tangible elements that create the rhythms and soul of

Day Five: Neighborhood store

the community. This observation process informs potential solutions so that they might remarry residents to the landscapes they inhabit.

Although it proposes an alternative design process, improvisation still operates within the tradition of environmental design. The principles of improvisation span the polarities of spontaneous change and formal composition. Alterations and transpositions are guided by individual expression in conjunction with social, environmental, and political analysis, traditional design strategies, and, most important, an understanding of common, everyday objects and practices (I refer to these as "the familiar"). The process begins with compositions that are formal but nonetheless free of programmatic constraints; the forms are silent, awaiting identity. Improvisation reshapes these design elements into new forms via the incremental transfer of ideas, producing familiar objects that reinforce the image of the community and extend existing traditions. The process of improvisation avoids hegemony, instead positioning the designer within a setting that demands creativity and conceptually collaborative thinking. As a method of inquiry, improvisation generates a new series of goals:

1. Adaptations that accommodate spontaneous change. The designer must accept as a given that cities and communities are in constant flux; spaces should encourage free individual and community expression.

2. Self-expression. The designer is not relegated to the role of facilitator or planner but offers formal interpretations.

3. Reinforcing the image of the community. The familiar validates the existence of multiple views of life in the city, even those that stand outside traditional or official discourses.

Day Five: Neighborhood store and watch tower

4. Extending and enriching the tradition of environmental design. Improvisation utilizes previous canons as points of departure but demands highly specific and individualized responses. It promotes change by concentrating on the collective and individual familiarity of pertinent components as they relate to a specific place or culture. For each design, the familiar must be uncovered. A familiar practice or object might be highly valued in one culture but completely irrelevant or nonexistent in another. The familiar has a dialogue with each design component, resulting in a design process structurally similar to the composition of jazz music. Design elements act as rhythms, combining and restructuring elements and spaces in a search for familiarity of place and culture. Within the boundary of the site, multiple responses layer to create a new set of familiar objects that function through

their interrelationships and uses as well as through the meanings users attach to them. New forms, elements, and patterns informed by historical, observational, and sociological analysis are derived from particular practices that reflect specific attitudes and values over time.

Many of the Durant Minipark innovations I've proposed here fall outside normative societal attitudes about what constitutes and is appropriate for neighborhoods and open space. They validate activities and events without judgmental strings attached. In 1965 Kevin Lynch wrote: "We should design for diversity, experiment with new types, open recreational choices, fit opportunities to the real diversity."[12] The miniparks of West Oakland await these opportunities. These diaries illuminate some of the hard questions that must be asked if open spaces are

12 Lynch, IMAGE OF THE CITY, 197.

Final version of the Street

to respond to diversity and play a role in the lives of the residents they aim to serve, whether in West Oakland or any other urban place. With my research, I make no claims to have solved the problems I've addressed; rather, I have made them visible. From my West Oakland observations, I formulated a set of questions, inquiries that must be pursued by any designer approaching open public spaces in urban areas:

1. In this era of standardization, how can we reflect and serve diversity in the landscape?

2. Can open spaces help to save neighborhoods facing economic, social, and physical decline?

3. Is nonjudgmental design possible?

4. By understanding different cultural patterns and practices, can new meanings emerge in the landscape?

5. Can physical design solutions continue to transform and reshape themselves as their surroundings transform?

The Diaries Continue.

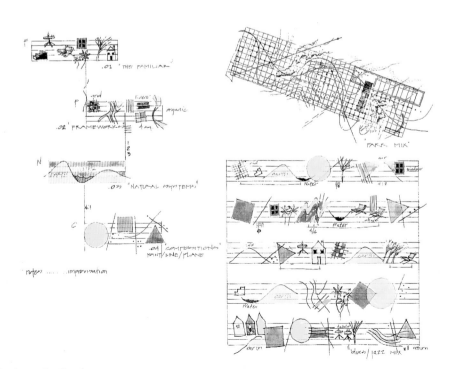

The improvisational process

MARGARET CRAWFORD AND JOHN KALISKI

QUOTIDIAN
BRICOLAGE

During 1993 and 1994, we taught a series of design studios at the Southern California Institute of Architecture (SCI-Arc). In these studios, we attempted to create an alternative design pedagogy based on everyday life. The studio projects were located in mundane urban settings, places that are invisible in the academic design discourse: fading 1950s suburbs, urban highway strips, dilapidated downtowns, and shopping malls that were neither failing nor particularly vibrant. By adopting a series of allegorical roles, students uncovered in these sites the mythic aspect hidden in the everyday. Revisiting the same locales successively as tourists, flaneurs, detectives, somnambulists, and bricoleurs, they discovered and constructed multiple layers of meaning. Rethinking these ordinary settings led them to transform the places into active sites, receptive to human experience and imagination.

Los Angeles River Improvements

Michael Ferguson, SCI-Arc, 1993

Site: *Right-of-way of the Los Angeles River*

This project creates a series of events in an otherwise neglected river channel, allowing it to be inhabited. A proposed public library pulls pedestrians in from the busy street and entices them to explore the concrete riverbanks. A café as well as a wading area shaded by the freeway brings more life to the riverbank. Movies are projected onto the freeway wall, creating an outdoor theater. Farther down the river, a pedestrian bridge crosses both river and freeway, linking a shopping mall with a residential neighborhood.

Culver City Bus Stops
Mahnaz Zahiry, SCI-Arc, 1994
Site: Culver City's buses and bus stops

This project treats the public bus system as a separate physical and social arena overlaid on the street network. Painted distinctive colors, the buses and bus stops are color-coded to indicate bus routes. Each bus shelter has amenities that encourage interaction and make use of time spent waiting. These include newsstands, coffee carts, key shops, and pay phones. Overheard stories and conversations are retold on billboards and panels inside the buses.

Studio Drive-In

Michael Stebbins, SCI-Arc, 1994

Site: *Abandoned drive-in movie theater in Culver City, California, bounded by a busy boulevard, a strip mall, and a residential neighborhood*

This project draws upon a series of Culver City–based ideas, artifacts, and events, including the city's rancho past, its motto, "Heart of Screenland," and Los Angeles car culture. The Studio Drive-In is a multiuse recreational facility with an outdoor revival cinema and classic cars for rent in which to view the movies. Sports amenities include pitch 'n' putt golf, tennis, volleyball, and in-line skating. Gardens on the site include a Rita Hayworth memory field (she is buried in a nearby cemetery), gigantic board games, and topiary livestock. A mini-mall with a restaurant, bar, bookstore, and outdoor terraces overlooks the restored movie screen.

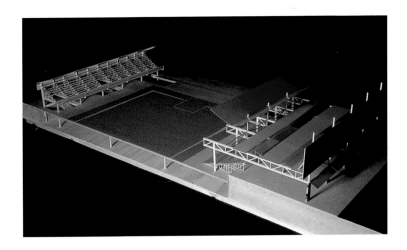

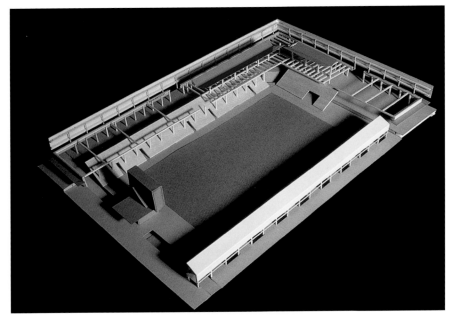

The Mercado

John Zorich, SCI-Arc, 1994

Site: Low-income area along Long Beach Boulevard in Long Beach, California

The Mercado integrates two different facilities—an open-air vendor market and a grassy field—to produce a new type of neighborhood center. The retail anchor has been replaced by a multiuse recreation field. The field can accommodate an open-air swap meet or a soccer game, changing according to the seasons and the activities and needs of the community. For both events, food vendors take over the spaces underneath the bleachers. When not in use, the field serves as a place for local residents and their families to gather, picnic, play, and converse.

customers and staff s

Studio Village Shopping Center Retrofit
Kari Overvik, SCI-Arc, 1994
Site: *Strip mall with big-box retail stores in Culver City, California*

In a semiprivate area between stores and the adjoining neighborhood, a series of small structures has been added to a shopping center in order to provide amenities for employees and local residents. Behind the Target store, a gate in the wall creates a private pedestrian entrance for local residents.

A small outdoor café and lunchroom is a pleasant place for both workers and residents. A stairwell leads to a day-care center on the roof. In the asphalt parking lot, a grassy island serves as a picnic area and shelter for those waiting for buses that have been rerouted to pass through the center.

Urban Social Condenser

Stephen Engblom, University of California, San Diego, 1992

Site: Center City East, a mixed commercial and industrial area on the fringes of downtown San Diego

A four-level parking garage has been adapted to accommodate multiple uses, bringing together different local groups. The main facility on the site is an adult vocational school that provides training for the area's unemployed. Bays for teaching auto mechanics are placed slightly below grade so that they are visible to passersby. Above are two floors of parking and, in the front of the building, a child-care center with a rooftop playground. A prefabricated chrome diner is inserted into the front of the building, providing a round-the-clock venue for students, teachers, and parents as well as for customers from all over the city.